One Day at a Time

One Day at a Time

An Inspirational Story of Fighting MS
with Hope and Attitude

David M. Sloan

*For my angelic wife and soul mate forever.
Andrea, you are an amazing woman.*

*And to Sydney and Jacob: your independent,
outgoing personalities and stellar achievements
inspire me. I am so proud of you!*

CONTENTS

PREFACE

Attitudes

Words can never adequately convey the incredible impact of our attitude toward life. The longer I live, the more convinced I become that life is 10 percent what happens to us and 90 percent how we respond to it.

I believe the single most significant decision I can make on a day-to-day basis is my choice of attitude. It is more important than my past, my education, my bankroll, my successes or failures, fame or pain, what other people think of me or say about me, my circumstances, or my position.

Attitude keeps me going or cripples my progress. It alone fuels my fire or assaults my hope. When my attitudes are right, there's no barrier too high, no valley too deep, no dream too extreme, no challenge too great for me.

-Chuck Swindoll

1

AN EYE OPENER

I'm sitting at Frutti's, sipping açaí with other hopefuls from our pousada. We're talking about John of God and his bizarre healing modalities. When we first arrived in Abadiânia, I drove my scooter to The Casa and heard screaming on a TV in the Main Hall. On the screen, John of God stood in trance as he grabbed a scalpel and cut something out of a person's eye without any anesthesia. I stared in disbelief. The video advanced and John of God forced a hemostat through someone's nose and pulled out a fatty tumor. Gross. Could this be real? The people from my office thought I was nuts traveling to Brazil by myself, but I didn't care. They could not appreciate my internal motivation for wanting to walk again. I'm the kind of guy who loves risk. My life has always been geared toward taking the toughest route to achieve the highest goals. Nothing came easy to me but I liked working hard in order to succeed. Negotiating major merger and acquisition (M&A) deals with corporate buyers and being a player in the oil and gas industry – that was easy. Healing myself from multiple sclerosis (MS) presented the type of outcome most people called unlikely or impossible. Since I've got MS, I'm going to win with my two secret weapons: hope and attitude.

The conversation with the other hopefuls went down many different paths. All discussions focused around healing. Vicki talked about a book written by Rasha. Her description of the book forced me to open my mind to the world of healing, spirituality and how reality manifested itself through body vibrations. What are body vibrations? I felt totally out of my comfort zone with unfamiliar vocabulary and unscientific concepts without empirical evidence. I forced myself to let go of my engineering education and methodical thought processes. The voice in the back of my head said, "Keep an open mind. Enjoy this fascinating experience. Listen and learn. Look around at where you are – so primitive yet so magical. Feel the energy from all these people who want the same thing."

A physician at our table discussed excerpts from "The Power of Now: A Guide to Spiritual Enlightenment" by Eckhart Tolle. Tom explained that living in the now was the truest path to happiness and enlightenment. As I wrote down these authors and book titles, my excitement grew. I felt overwhelmed by the possibility that something wonderful would happen to me in Brazil. While I still could not grasp the concept of spirituality, my body became energized to let go of my structured world and embrace the unknown. This town gave me hope about the possibilities and alternatives to feel better. This town and its community of people gave me strength to believe in my ability to heal.

Everyone shared his or her experiences at the Casa. We had arrived on Monday the previous week. The Casa and João de Deus (John of God) are only available to visitors Wednesday through Friday. Wayne asked everyone at the table, "Why did you come here? What do you want to accomplish?" Before I could respond, Valerie bent over and whispered in my ear that I needed to meet a woman named Patti Conklin. I made a mental note to ask her more about this lady. Later, Valerie excitedly tapped me on the arm. "There goes Patti Conklin walking down the road towards The Casa. Let me go see if she will join us."

The next thing I knew Patti Conklin was sitting next to me. I vaguely remembered reading about her in a book written by the guide of our group, Josie Ravenwing, entitled, "The Book of Miracles: The Healing Work of João de Deus". We both said hi and exchanged pleasantries. Being inquisitive and somewhat skeptical, I asked her what she did for a living. Patti said, "I'm a Medical Intuitive".

"What does that mean? I've never heard that job title before. I'm totally confused." In my head I also questioned whether I sat next to a charlatan. Patti told me she saw people differently than me. "When you look at a person, you see them with a face and personality. When I see a person, I see the energies in their body. I look directly into the body and see its physical and energetic workings. Whereas you see a face, I see a television screen with snow," Patti patiently described to me.

"I still don't get it. Give me an example," I insist.

"OK," she said. "When I look at you I can tell that you have seven lesions on your brain and two on your spinal cord and that your disease manifested from a traumatic event that happened when you were six years old." Wow! I looked down at the ground as my eyes lost focus. Still, I felt skeptical. How could she know? It took me a few minutes to process her words. I closed my eyes and looked inside my mind at the memories of my childhood. Then it hit me. Goose bumps sprouted all over my arms. I had never met this woman before. Nor had I told her anything about my medical condition. Shortly after our encounter, Patti mentioned she needed to leave but looked forward to meeting me again.

Evenings at The Casa grounds were peaceful. Some people walked through the buildings while others cruised to the covered lookout veranda for meditation. Using my international calling card on one of the two pay phones at The Casa grounds, I found Andrea, Sydney and Jacob eating dinner. I called every other day to share my most recent experiences. After speaking with the kids, Andrea and I discussed my incredible activities over the last few days. I mentioned meeting Patti Conklin and what she said to me about seeing my body differently. I tried to summarize what Patti told me. "She said she could see seven lesions on my brain and two on my spinal cord and that my disease manifested from a traumatic event that happened when I was six years old."

"You told me you were six years old when the accident happened with your eye." Andrea reminded me.

"Oh yeah. How could she know about my eye? I can't wait to hear what the MRI technician sees on my brain when I return to the States." My mind had a hard time comprehending how a stranger knew so much about me. I shook my head in disbelief as I hung up the telephone.

It's 1967. My parents took me to a Woolworth's store at an outdoor mall in St. Louis. After leaving the store, I bounced down the sidewalk on a big rubber Romper Room Punch-A-Ball. The punch-a-ball was a large, heavy, bead-filled balloon with a thick rubber handle attached to it. You could either punch the ball in the air making noise as the beads collided against the outer rubber lining or ride on top of the ball bouncing in random directions.

After returning home, I played inside with my new toy and kept crashing onto the floor and into our family room furniture. My dad yelled at me. "You're driving me crazy. Take that ball outside on the patio near the kitchen so your brother can watch." The flowerbed closest to the house was filled with budding rose bushes. My one-year old younger brother, Steven, watched me through the glass-screened storm door. He held onto the door for balance with the palms of his little hands.

I bounced the ball in the air watching my little brother smile through the glass door. He kept springing up and down with his legs. The handle was sturdy enough to use both hands to bounce the ball in different directions. Unfortunately I punched the ball towards the rose bushes. The rubber collided with a thorn and the ball exploded. The differential in air pressure between the ball and the outdoor air caused the explosion. The beads from inside the ball thrust into my right eye. Blood flew everywhere. I screamed loudly and out of control. My mom ran outside and pressed a dishtowel against my eye to help contain the bleeding. The dishtowel looked old and worn with a plaid design on a gray background. Not for long. By the time we reached the Emergency Room at Children's Hospital, the dishtowel was soaked in my blood.

Soon after entering the Emergency Room, my mom passed out. I heard someone shout they needed to find her a bed. The hospital made an emergency page to an eye specialist named Dr. Jack Hartstein. Within the hour he entered the Emergency Room dressed in a tuxedo. We had interrupted a charity event. After he completed his work in the operating room, the nurses admitted me onto the pediatric trauma floor with patches over both eyes. "He needs time to heal. David may never be able to see again out of his right eye. I would expect him to be in the hospital at least two weeks," the doctor calmly told my parents.

How could Patti Conklin know about this traumatic event? Maybe she really could read people's emotional, physical and spiritual vibrations. If she can see this in me, maybe she can help me heal. That single encounter gave me new hope towards feeling better and walking again. I needed to spend more time with this woman.

2

AREN'T YOU
THE AMBITIOUS ONE

After the accident, my parents did everything they could to protect my eyes and me. I had to stay far away from fireworks displays in friends' back yards. No more roughhousing with my brothers. Everything I did or wanted to do required their approval. Did this protectiveness create my ambitious, independent and overachiever mentality? I had to prove to them I could succeed away from their protective control. My response to their cautious behavior towards me caused me to choose a degree, college and career that took them by surprise. Petroleum engineering? Austin, Texas? My mom commented by saying, "Only you, David. I know you can do it. Your positive attitude towards everything you touch will take you far in life." My relationship with my mom always felt different after almost losing my eye. We connected. Our bond felt stronger than a typical mother-son connection. We had very special and personal discussions together. She always asked me to help her cook dinner and bake cookies. She had confidence in my ability to succeed. Only through the passage of time would I fully appreciate our commonality.

After college, I worked in my dream job as a drilling engineer until oil prices collapsed. Eighteen months post graduation Amoco eliminated my position. Economic conditions forced me to ask myself, "What should I do now?" There were no available jobs in the oil industry. I had to reinvent myself. My attitude waned but reality forced me to start over in the financial services industry. I knew I could succeed as a stockbroker. Within six months of earning my securities licenses, the stock market crashed. A voice in the back of head screamed at me. "Stay positive. Your life is a journey. Nothing ever comes easy to you. Create your own success. Don't give up. Fight back!"

Soon after my personal pep talk, Andrea and I met. On one of our frequent hot summer days in Dallas, we attended an afternoon pool party at one of her nursing friends' houses. Andrea worked at a new job as a nurse in the operating room at Medical City and looked forward to building friendships with fellow workers. It was a great day to be outside. The music blared, cold beers flowed, and everyone had fun. After I hopped out of the pool and dried off, I joined a crowd inside for Jell-O shots. Soon after the crowd became loud and rambunctious, the husband of the host yelled at the top of his lungs, "Excuse me. Everyone pay attention. I want to make an announcement. Stop dripping water from the pool in the house." Hearing this caused me to make one of my sarcastic, comedic comments to the crowd. "It sounds like I'm being lectured by my parents!" Everyone laughed. About that same time Andrea stepped into the bathroom down the hallway. Much to her surprise, when she returned to the bar, a friend told us we had to immediately leave. The owner came out of his bedroom with a gun in his hand. We were quickly ushered out of their house; the party was over. Andrea looked at me with hate in her eyes because I embarrassed her. "I didn't do anything wrong," I replied. It didn't matter. We had to leave. The car ride home was uncomfortably quiet. Once home, all I could say was, "I didn't do anything wrong. I'm going on a bike ride." That was a fight not worth fighting. I really liked Andrea and did not want to jeopardize our relationship with a trivial fight over something so silly. In every situation that included a disagreement with Andrea, I always walked away without terse or negative words from me. For the first time in my life, Andrea helped me understand the meaning of love. I wanted this relationship to work.

I spent the rest of the afternoon riding my 12-speed bike twice around White Rock Lake. I must have pushed myself too hard. The next day my neck really hurt and my finger pads were numb. Every time I lowered my head, it felt like my neck short-circuited with electricity running through my arms. Being a typical male, I assumed my health would improve over time. After one week with no improvement, Andrea convinced me to call my doctor. He recommended an MRI. Before the test, I informed the MRI technician my mother had MS. "Please let me know if you see any signs of the disease," I begged the technician. The next day my doctor called me and said the MRI showed I had a bulging disk in my neck. "David, the MRI showed no signs of MS. Go buy yourself a neck brace and wear it for 3-4 weeks," my doctor reported. I wore the brace for a week before removing it. The stiffness and pain from wearing the brace created more symptoms than it solved.

While my neck pain alleviated, my finger pads continued to be numb. Other strange symptoms developed that gave me reason to pause and wonder why. Whenever I sat or stood to urinate, there was a considerable delay before voiding. My urologist told me these symptoms were normal for an adult male my age. Fatigue caused me to get really tired as each day got longer. Maybe I worked too much. I thought to myself, "Every American worked too many hours for too little compensation. Was I really any different?" Paranoia consumed my thoughts. Why were all of these doctors telling me I'm fine while my body told me to be concerned? The afternoon pool party, subsequent gun episode and the stress filled bike ride proved to mark a significant date in my life. It only took seven more years to understand and appreciate its true significance. Our active lifestyles helped me to ignore all of these cryptic signals.

In 1991 I married the love of my life. Three years later, Andrea and I were blessed with our healthy daughter Sydney. The birth of a child changed our perspective on many things. Andrea and I decided it was more important for her to be a stay-at-home mom than work and use childcare. We focused on being stellar parents. We read to Sydney every night. We bought all of the latest home safety equipment and an endless supply of toys and stuffed animals. Why not? Sydney was daddy's little girl. She deserved the best we could afford. When Andrea stopped working, our expenses increased while our income declined. What did we expect? I felt the pressure increase every month as my paycheck barely paid our bills. While financially uncomfortable, we had no second thoughts about Andrea staying home with Sydney. I could see the special mother-daughter bond develop and saw the glow of happiness in both of their faces.

My career was poised to become even more rewarding – and exciting. My job provided me with a decent salary plus bonus potential based upon the success of our firm. I was doing well financially but wanted more. Two non-working mouths to feed motivated me to want more. I became a specialist in helping companies rationalize non-strategic oil and gas properties. My responsibilities included preparing the property sale memorandum, managing the data room process, marketing the properties/companies and negotiating the purchase and sale agreements. After more than four years of supporting other executives within our firm, I felt ready to take on a larger business development role. "Bring in new business and your bonus could be larger," the owner informed me. Those were exactly the words I needed to hear. The ability to earn more money based on my efforts motivated me like nothing else could.

That same year I was asked to join an adjunct committee for The University of Texas at Austin's (UT Austin's) Petroleum Engineering Department. They wanted to explore revising their curriculum to include finance and accounting classes. I brought a younger, biased perspective since I had obtained my MBA and worked as an investment banker using these courses on a daily basis. My efforts and input were well rewarded. I was invited to give the closing remarks at UT Austin's College of Engineering Spring 1995 commencement. What a cool experience speaking in front of more than 5,000 people at the Sam Erwin Center. Both Andrea and my dad attended. Later they expressed how proud they were of me.

My business development efforts provided me with access to decision makers in oil and gas companies. I met with presidents, chief financial officers and vice presidents of acquisitions to discuss their buying and selling decisions. Concurrently, my company began documentation for creating an institutional equity fund. Our firm planned to manage approximately $100 million of insurance company capital for direct investments into oil and gas projects. Unfortunately, our management did not invite me to participate. They did not agree with me that everyone's interest at our firm should be aligned with the same objective towards success. By removing that potential monetary reward, they gave me reason to look elsewhere for a better job opportunity.

While traveling independently in search of new business mandates and managing existing client divestitures, Andrea and I were blessed with the birth of Jacob. Approximately four weeks after his birth, he developed an infection that sent him to Children's Medical Center. Fortunately, Andrea knew how to communicate with the pediatric doctors and other hospital providers. As I watched the 1996 Super Bowl in Jacob's hospital room, I negotiated with a headhunter on an opportunity to open the Houston office for Canada's largest investment bank. This company also owned a premier oil and gas lending operation. They wanted to open a U.S. investment banking office and focus on leveraging their existing banking relationships. Their vision included developing senior-level relationships with American companies for both domestic investment banking and Canadian cross-border M&A opportunities. My acquisition and divestiture expertise provided a perfect match with one of their senior bankers who wanted to cross over into investment banking. After seven months of interviews in Calgary, Chicago and Toronto they hired me to co-found their new office.

My ambition to earn more money motivated me to find this new job. My ambition to want more responsibility caused me to reach out for a new challenge. My ambition and obsessive-compulsive behavior drove me to keep searching until I found the best opportunity for my family and me. Only later would I know if our decision turned out to be a good decision. Someone once told me if you never play the lottery, you can't win. I wanted to play, and I wanted to win.

3

HOUSTON – WE HAVE A PROBLEM

Changing jobs and moving to Houston turned into a wonderful motivator. I had confidence in my ability to succeed and reap the monetary rewards of my additional responsibilities. What I failed to consider was how the combination of heat, humidity and stress would wreak havoc on my body. My new responsibilities consumed every minute of every working hour. I thought I knew about being busy and working hard. It never crossed my mind what that really meant. Welcome to my new reality.

As my sister-in-law Laura used to tell me, I was the epitome of a fired-up guy. New job excitement and playing in the major leagues of investment banking caused my attitude to soar. Opening a new office for Canada's largest investment bank was a monumental task. I learned a new level of office politics and corporate diplomacy. But most important was the level of responsibility and access my job brought to me. I thought I had access with my previous employer. Now I created and presented M&A ideas to chairmen, presidents and chief financial officers. They rewarded us with new corporate finance business for bringing them good ideas.

My days grew more and more busy as we built our company's name recognition and reputation for stellar ideas. I hunted for business development opportunities, created new M&A ideas, and competed to win corporate finance business for our new franchise. This was no small feat in the world of significant competition. However, we offered a unique advantage over our competitors. We provided expertise in cross-border mergers and acquisitions between the U.S. and Canada before the concept became a routine alternative among U.S. energy companies. The Canadian dollar traded at approximately two-thirds the rate of the American dollar so American companies could buy Canadian oil and gas companies or assets at a substantial discount. We were educators. We helped American companies understand valuation and vernacular differences. It felt good to teach executives something they wanted and needed to know. Companies needed to grow either organically or through mergers and acquisitions. Corporate executives wanted to hear our cross border ideas. Life was good and getting better. Never in my wildest dreams could I imagine utilizing my undergraduate and graduate degrees coupled with my communication skills to get paid handsomely for my unique skill set.

All of the fun and excitement at work came with a price. Family. Many days we worked twelve, fifteen or eighteen hours. One time my colleagues and I finished editing a presentation at 3:00 AM, drove home, showered and boarded an early morning plane to present our ideas at an 11:00 AM meeting in Tulsa, Oklahoma. A typical week included two or three days of business development travel and three or four days of working late. Andrea was not happy with me never being home and always working late or traveling while she stayed home with two toddlers. She struggled to keep our family unit running smoothly. Two kids less than two years old kept her extremely busy. On a typical workday Andrea would call me around 4:00 PM and ask, "When are you going to be home? Let's have dinner tonight as a family." "That sounds good to me. I'll be home by 6:30 PM." At 6:15 PM I called and told her I would be 30 minutes late but home for dinner. At 7:30 PM I called again and told her to eat dinner without me. You could only imagine her tone of voice. I could feel her seething over the telephone. Another dinner eating from a Styrofoam box away from Andrea and the kids. My family ideals collided with my business responsibilities. It tore my insides apart. I loved my new job responsibilities but cringed at the resulting family tension.

One weekend in October we drove back to Dallas. We had not sold our house and needed to bring back some warmer clothing to Houston. The pressure from work, long hours and lack of activity on our house took its toll on my body. On our sole stop for lunch and gas, I noticed something strange. After gassing up the car, I walked inside the convenience store to pay. On the way back to our car, the

PROVIDED by YOUR JOKESTER MASTER FRIEND Michael Wade Hancey

JOKE –a- thon joke book

Q: Which vampire lives in a kitchen drawer?   **A:** Count Spatula!

Q: Why are noses with colds so fit?   **A:** Because they're always running!

Q: What kind of vegetable do you find in the gym?   **A:** Muscle sprouts!

Q: What did the sun say to the cloud when he went on vacation?   **A:** You'll be mist!

Q: Which famous sea creature never tidies his room?   **A:** The Loch Mess Monster!

Q: What kind of ice cream does Frankenstein eat?   **A:** Cookies 'n' scream!

Q: What did Mr. Volcano say to Mrs. Volcano when they got married?   **A:** "I lava you!"

GIGGLES joke book

Q: What kind of hat do birds wear?   A: A Robin Hood!

"Are you milking that cow in your new hat?"

"No, I'm using a pail."

Q: Why do cowboys turn their hats up on the side?

A: So that three of them can sit in the front in a pickup!

Q: What do cowboys put on their pancakes?   **A:** Maple Stirrup!

Q: What famous fish wears a red, white, and blue hat?   **A:** Uncle Salmon!

"I saw a sign in a restaurant that said 'Watch your coat and hat,' so I did and someone stole my dinner.

Q: What exercise do lazy people love to do?   **A:** Diddly-squats!

Q: What do you call fake spaghetti?   **A:** Im-pasta!

GIGGLES joke book

Jeweler: Hello, 911? I own a jewelry store and an elephant just walked in, sucked up all my jewelry with his trunk and ran away.

Police: Can you give me a description?

Jeweler: I can't really, because he had a nylon stocking over his head.

"Were you afraid when the robber pulled a knife on you?"

"No, I could see he wasn't a professional. The knife still had butter on it."

MY FRIEND,

Please take care and have a week that's excellent to the max in every way, shape, and form!!! I'll see you on Thursday!!!

tingling reappeared on the left side of my body. Why was my left foot dragging behind me? Nothing hurt inside so once again I dismissed another cryptic signal.

After we reached our house in Lake Highlands, we opened the front door and walked upstairs. Sydney and Jacob crawled up the stairs to our game room and dumped over a big bucket of toys. The kids played together quietly so I walked into the hall and pulled on the rope to our attic stairs. Within seconds, the stairs unfolded into our second floor hallway. I climbed the stairs and flipped on the light switch. After pulling myself up completely into the attic and avoiding the nails protruding from inside the roof, I began walking along the plywood flooring. The floor was narrow but offered an alternative to straddling the ceiling joists. Something didn't feel right. That's because my left foot was numb. Without any sensation in my foot, I stepped off the plywood. When I finally regained my balance, my left foot broke through the sheetrock ceiling in our second floor hallway. Insulation from inside the attic flew everywhere onto the hallway floor. What a mess. My heart pounded while the sweat gushed from my forehead. This was no incidental accident. Andrea yelled towards me, "What just happened? Are you alright?"

"I don't know. Maybe you should finish up here." I felt nauseous and dizzy and had to sit down. How could this happen to me? My mind raced with paranoia as I tried to comprehend the reason for my vertigo.

Upon returning to Houston, I immediately went to see my primary care physician (PCP). Why was my left foot numb and dragging? My PCP could not find anything wrong. "Take some muscle relaxers and see me in six months," he told me. Approximately twelve months passed. Work provided me with increasing financial rewards based on our office's success. Along with my personal success came increased stress. Andrea made every attempt to acclimate to Houston's humidity because she knew I loved my job. What a loyal and special woman!

Immediately after selling our house in Dallas, we bought a house in a great neighborhood with a pool. Once we moved in, Andrea built relationships with neighbors who also had kids of similar ages. We joined the Jewish Community Center so Sydney and Jacob could participate in physical activities like soccer and gymnastics. It finally started to feel like home. Andrea appeared happy. The kids and I had a special connection ritual when I pulled out of our garage towards the street. I would look into the kitchen window and we'd wave goodbye with our index fingers. Everyone would smile when I pulled away.

My company started throwing rewards at me because of our success. One of the rewards was a membership at an exclusive downtown health club. When did I have time to work out? However, I needed to make time to exercise and relieve some of my bottled-up stress. One day at the gym I attempted to use an elliptical machine. My legs felt weird when I tried to rotate the pedals in a circular movement when I pushed and pulled the arm grips. I felt shaky, off-balance and very unstable. Maybe I needed instructions from a personal trainer. After slowing the pedals to a stop, I walked over to a step-aerobics class and tried to follow the teacher's routine. Now my legs felt really strange – wobbly and tingly. What a waste of time. Time that I did not have. I walked quickly into the dressing room, dressed, and returned to work.

That afternoon, I told my secretary I would be out for several hours at a doctor's appointment. Sandy could feel the anxiety in my voice and looked concerned. After my PCP reviewed my symptoms, he was convinced I had ruptured a disk in my lower back that would require emergency surgery. A back x-ray proved him wrong. My spine looked perfectly intact. He suggested I see an orthopedic surgeon for a second opinion. This doctor took one look at my x-ray and said there was nothing for him to operate on. "Go see a physical therapist," he said condescendingly. Three weeks of PT did little to alleviate my concerns but the symptoms disappeared. More importantly, I did not have the time to waste by giving any more thought to this inconvenience.

In the summer of 1998, something felt terribly wrong. My body did not appreciate the ninety-degree plus days coupled with 92% humidity. I would walk out my door in the morning dressed in my power suit and immediately feel like I needed another shower. It was only 6:45 AM and the sweat poured from all pores in my body. More urgently, the tingling in my hands noticeably increased. I also lost all feeling in my feet. They were numb. To make matters worse, my lower extremities became very weak. What had caused my body's rebellion?

For the first time in many months, I left work early because my paranoia consumed my thoughts. After reading books to Sydney and

Jacob before bedtime, I walked off-balance down our steps. My shoulders bounced off the walls like pinballs in a pinball machine. I wanted to brush off these personal challenges; it had to go away. Andrea and I contemplated what to do next. We sat next to each other on our leather couch. She saw my fatigue and the dejected look on my face. "You need to go back to the doctor. Something's not right. I'm really worried about you."

"When? I don't have time to keep seeing doctors. We're right in the middle of selling a Canadian company. I leave for Calgary the day after tomorrow."

Andrea shook her head with a disappointed look on her face. Tears formed in the corners of her eyes. She paused before speaking softly. "David. Stop making excuses. You need to make time. Please. Do it for us."

By the end of the summer I agreed to go back to my doctor. The numbness and tingling prompted my PCP to suggest seeing a neurologist. I needed a label for my physical challenges. The neurologist had a sense for the culprit but didn't let me in on his little secret. He ordered a spinal tap. On the day of this procedure, the nurse instructed me to lie flat for several hours after they stuck the four-inch needle into my spinal cord. The following day my head pounded so badly that Andrea and the kids needed to whisper around me. The music in the car sounded louder than the loudest concert. Apparently the hole where they pulled spinal fluid never closed and leaked spinal fluid. Andrea rushed me back to the hospital. Within minutes of injecting blood into my spinal cord below the area of the spinal tap, the headaches stopped. I learned a new concept – blood patch. Although the headaches discontinued, the results of the spinal tap proved negative. This experience created a new level of aggravation and torture without any answers.

My neurologist recommended an MRI. He also wanted to see the MRI taken in 1990 after overexerting myself on the bike ride in Dallas. In order to minimize my time away from work, the MRI test began at 9:00 pm. After finishing the first draft of our latest M&A presentation, I walked into my partner's office. At 8:15 PM, I closed Mark's door. "Mark, I need to leave early tonight. Don't be alarmed, but something doesn't feel right in my body. I've tried to hide my symptoms and pretend everything would be OK. No more lies to myself. No more hiding from the truth. Andrea convinced me to dig deeper and find the answer through an MRI." Mark's answer gave me reassurance. "You know me better than anyone but my wife. We spend more time together, that's for sure. I'll cover for you. David, stop and remember you and your family come first. Get out of here and take care of yourself."

After several days of analysis by the radiologist, my neurologist asked me to come in for a follow-up visit. The good news was I finally had a label for my symptoms. The bad news was I had MS. The neurologist pulled out the MRI films from 1990. The doctor drew circles on the film. "See these spots on the film, they are MS. The radiologist misdiagnosed the numbness in your fingers." My anger raged about that doctor's incompetence. I always believed doctors were placed on a pedestal. When they formed an opinion and made a diagnosis, it had to be right. I disproved my own myth. How could the radiologist miss those spots? They looked obvious to me.

Immediately following my diagnosis I shared the discouraging news with my dad on a 30-minute phone call. We spoke weekly, because he always wanted an update on his grandkids. "Dad, how's it going? Do you have a few minutes?"

"What's wrong? Are Andrea and the kids OK?"

"They're really good. Unfortunately I'm not. My neurologist just told me I have MS."

"Oh my God. Please tell me you're joking."

"I wish I could. The shock factor hasn't sunk in yet but I'm sad and afraid that I could wind up like mom."

I knew this wasn't going to be a pleasant conversation. My dad lived with my mom's disease since 1980. That was the year our family's neurologist provided my mom with her MS label. Unfortunately the doctor called her form of the disease "chronic progressive MS". The disease never stopped progressing, eventually immobilizing both legs and her left arm. The end result for my parents was financially ruinous. My dad tried to take care of my mom at home for almost thirteen years. Once she became completely immobile, my dad reluctantly made the decision to transfer her to a nursing home. Once he could no longer afford to pay after exhausting all of their modest savings, my mom became a ward of the state on Medicaid.

When hearing this story, people shook their heads and questioned the fairness of life. Not my mom. She always let people know she felt lucky. "There are lots of people who would be happy to trade places," she would say. "I can see, I can hear and I have family and friends that love me and come to visit me. And, besides, who would want to visit a grouch...someone who cries and complains? I certainly wouldn't." My mother was a true inspiration to lots of people. Attitude alleviated her burden on a daily basis. My mom inspired me to imitate her attitude and hope for a better day.

Thus the head games began. Thoughts in my mind fast forwarded to seeing me laid up in a nursing home bed like my mom. "Stop". The voice in the back of my head screamed at me. "That alternative is unacceptable. You will not let this disease ruin your family. You need to become proactive about your health." My dad and I also made the conscientious decision to hide my condition from my mom. She didn't need to hear this news and beat herself up while lying in bed every day. Our decision haunted me. I lived the lie but knew it couldn't last forever. I wouldn't let it last forever.

Within 30 days after my diagnosis I began injecting one of the "ABC" drugs. In 1998, there were three FDA approved medications for people diagnosed with relapsing remitting MS – Avonex, Betaseron, and Copaxone. Each injectable drug used different molecular formulas to slow the progression of the disease and increase the time between attacks.

After receiving a second opinion, my diagnosis did not change but the type of drug therapy did change. After calming down from my anger and denial I settled back into my workaholic tendencies. My firm won the sale mandate of King Ranch Energy (KRE) based on my relationship with senior executives of the company and significant divestiture expertise.

After watching the 1998 Super Bowl, my partner and I traveled to Denver on an initial marketing trip of KRE. We initiated acquisition discussions with a number of potential public company candidates. KRE wanted stock as their preferred compensation because of tax implications. The stress from late nights working on the Sales Memorandum and constant traveling created new symptoms of my disease. My left foot started dragging whenever I walked. While trying to ignore this latest inconvenience, the voice in my head told me something had to change. Something dramatic needed to change.

4

MY FIRST MAJOR DECISION

Attitude had always played an important role for me during my career progression. But never did I connect the dots between attitude and health. Quickly I learned about the direct connection. As long as I stayed positive and fought to overcome my personal challenges, I knew in my heart my health would improve. My mind migrated from a fearless, immortal, ambitious individual to someone who had no choice but to accept the inconvenience of this disease called MS. Why did my attitude sleep through this nightmare? Sometimes I really wondered. I changed my diet, exercised three times every week, stayed positive and very hopeful. Yet my condition continued to regress. Something had to change.

My workload increased on the KRE transaction. I thought my days were full while I gave my complete attention to their deal. Not for long. By early spring, one of our Canadian clients received a hostile takeover offer from a US-based oil and gas company. In Canada, a 21-day clock started ticking immediately upon receipt of a hostile takeover. On day 21 either the original bidder or a white knight owned the company. Since I had the most capacity to take on another assignment, I commuted between Houston and Calgary for the takeover transaction with stopovers in Denver where the majority of the KRE prospective buyers had headquarters. Sleep became an afterthought. Stress and fatigue became my two worst enemies. One night while evaluating the economics of certain merger candidates in Houston, the fatigue overtook my ability to think rationally. I looked at my boss and one of the Managing Directors from our Calgary office and told them I needed to leave. They looked at me with intense disappointment. "You can't leave," they barked at me. But I did, without hesitation. Up until that moment I had managed to ignore my symptoms. For the first time since my diagnosis Andrea questioned my commitment towards my health. "Can you really continue at your pace and ignore the response from your body? Wake up and look at yourself. You are self-destructing."

One night while lying in bed wide-awake I asked myself, "Should I stay or should I go? How important is making money? Could I walk away from my dream job? I am self-destructing working too much and living in the heat and humidity of Houston." It took several sleepless nights of contemplating my health and my job. Andrea was the only person who heard me outwardly speak these thoughts. My attitude stayed strong but my body would not cooperate. My ambition could not keep pace with my physical limitations. I reluctantly concluded my health took priority over how much money I earned. What an earth shattering realization. My immortality, or should I say lack of immortality rocked my attitude. How could I walk away from my career and educational background because of my health? It took several weeks of closed-door conversations with Mark. He knew we succeeded because we worked well as a team. He knew it hurt me to give in to this brutal disease. But Mark also saw the devastating impact of MS from his next-door neighbor. She lived in Houston in the cooler months and moved to Seattle every summer to escape the devastating swamp-like conditions in Houston. My age and pressure from being the sole money earner forced me to remember my primary responsibilities - my health and three other mouths to feed.

Once we decided to leave the heat and humidity of Houston, we had to determine where to move. We knew that heat and humidity were the number one and two enemies of MS. Alaska was cool with low humidity. Too far away and too cold. California sounded good but we didn't know anyone who lived there and the cost of living appeared unreasonable. What about Denver? The climate in the Denver area offered one of our country's best-kept secrets. My research showed the humidity in Denver normally stayed below 20% - less than one-fourth the humidity in Houston. Most people thought it snowed a lot in Denver with brutally cold temperatures. We quickly learned that Denver had 300 plus days of sunshine every year. When it did snow, it usually melted the next day. Denver sounded good and I spent a lot of time in the city anyway on the KRE transaction. How convenient. Now we had a good idea of where we wanted to move.

The next questions for me to answer – What kind of work offered lower stress and paid descent wages? Where do I start finding opportunities and interviews?

One of my best friends from graduate school lived in Denver. Whenever I traveled to Denver, we tried to connect after work. He recently became frustrated with his job as a consultant in the construction industry. One of his former roommates became the president of an insurance brokerage company owned by his family. An insurance broker provided the role of an intermediary between a company who needed to buy insurance and the insurance company who wanted to sell them insurance. Doug joined the firm in charge of building their local construction practice. "You should interview with us," he suggested. My first reaction did not surprise him. I knew nothing about the insurance industry. "Neither did I," Doug replied. "We need people who understand their industry. We have account executives that know insurance but don't have industry expertise. You certainly know a lot about oil and gas. They can teach you what you need to know about insurance. And by the way, we're currently interviewing for an oil and gas producer."

Once we made the decision to move, preferably in Denver, I needed to find the right job match. I had spent the last twelve years in sales. The perfect opportunity for me would be to use my technical background coupled with my ability to sell. While I recognized I was not going to replicate a job with earning potential like investment banking, I still wanted to control my ability to earn more than a salary only paycheck.

Insurance brokerage for oil and gas companies appealed to me. Doug presented an opportunity to utilize my senior level relationships across the country. I took advantage of being in Denver for several meetings with KRE candidates to interview for the insurance broker position. My interview went really well. Within one week of the interview they called to inform me they hired a local person for the job. He had run the risk management department for an oil and gas company. Before their call, I anticipated the job offer and had mentally already moved. This experience humbled me and provided a large blow to my confidence. I wanted that job in Denver. I needed to remind myself to learn from that interview and not give up. So where do I go from here?

Several weeks later, the president of Doug's company called me again. "We really like your background. Even though we filled the oil and gas producer position, we want you to join our firm in a newly created job. I see the merger and acquisition market heating up and I want you to provide insurance solutions to facilitate M&A transactions. What do you think?" he asked. How cool. They had recognized my unique background and had created a job for me. Sign me up. I knew nothing about the insurance products used to solve transactional problems such as lack of environmental indemnification, litigation buyouts and representation & warranty contractual issues. However, I did know how to communicate with attorneys, corporate executives and other investment bankers discussing how to help them close deals and earn their success fees.

Several months passed while negotiating my compensation and moving expenses. The spring and summer months crushed me physically and mentally with the heat and humidity in Houston. Mentally I already made the decision it was not if we were going to move, but when were we going to move. My expectations continued to grow regarding the job in Denver. Everything seemed right. The weather certainly appeared easier to tolerate. The humidity was much lower and every time I traveled there the temperature felt cooler with a much lower heat index. More importantly I felt better whenever I spent time in Denver.

It was early summer before they verbally offered me the job. The verbal offer provided us comfort in knowing we had a place to hang our hats in Denver. The offer also gave us enough confidence to place our house on the market. A verbal agreement was nice but I wanted and needed an offer in writing before resigning from my current job.

The written offer finally arrived in early July. What a relief. I created this opportunity because I knew it would lead me towards feeling better. Let my healing journey begin! Wait a minute, slow down. How could I resign in the middle of the most important M&A transaction of my career before completing the transaction? We were far enough into the deal to know the transaction should close since KRE just executed a Letter of Intent with a Denver based company. Would I really walk away from a significant bonus? Based on the way I physically felt and the excitement towards moving to Denver, the money just didn't matter to me. For the first time in my life, I made a decision from my heart instead of my head.

Early one evening after most people already left our building, I walked over to my boss's office. Sylvia was the hardest working woman I ever met. She had a major advantage – unmarried and loved to work late. When I approached her office, I could smell the acrid cigarette smoke in the air. We worked in a non-smoking building but she didn't care, especially after normal working hours.

I walked into her office and closed the door. My stomach tightened. This was going to be a tough conversation for me. "Hey Sylvia, do you have a few minutes?" She opened her desk drawer, pulled out an empty Altoids can and stamped out her cigarette. Her eyes opened wide with curiosity.

"We need to talk about my future with our group. By now, I'm sure you've heard about my health challenges. You have been very generous and fair with the meteoric rise in my career. Unfortunately I can't keep up with you or this lifestyle anymore. My disease coupled with Houston's heat and humidity created too many problems for me. I just don't feel good here. Remember when I walked out of that meeting with you and Drew? It really sucks to leave. After much debate, Andrea and I decided I needed to focus on improving my health. With much remorse, I am tendering my resignation."

Sylvia told me she knew about my health and how tough this decision had to be for me. After her last words, she broke down and cried. Never before had I seen anyone, especially my boss, show such emotion. I sat across from her in disbelief. What a moving experience. I didn't know what to say next. We both sat in silence for several minutes – several long minutes. Sylvia broke the silence. "We are really going to miss you and your great M&A ideas. I have no regrets about hiring you. Your tenacity, attention to detail, work ethic and incredible energy helped make our office fun, successful and rewarding. You need to take care of yourself. While I hate to admit it, you are making the right decision."

When I stood up and steadied myself by holding both arms of the chair, the last three years passed before my eyes. I worked so hard to reach this pinnacle in my career. With one long and tearful goodbye, I readied myself for my next journey. While it was tough to accept my new reality, deep in my heart I knew I made the right decision with no regrets. How can you argue with someone who puts his health and family before his career? My priorities became very clear. Do whatever it takes to feel better, get stronger and avoid the unacceptable alternative. While my attitude wavered, I felt very positive about good things to come. On one hand I couldn't believe I was about to walk away from my dream job; on the other hand I needed to heal and begin the next chapter in my life.

5

BEING SELF-CONSCIOUS

Moving to Denver was an easy decision. My thoughts filled with excitement. Andrea and the kids wanted to live in Denver and enjoy the Rocky Mountains. I looked forward to the challenge of meeting new people, learning a new profession, and feeling better. I knew nothing about corporate insurance or insurance to facilitate M&A transactions but I had confidence in my ability to learn quickly and succeed. We decided to build a new house, which we passionately visited on a daily basis to watch the builders' progress. Our foresight to find a model home with a first floor master bedroom proved to be genius planning to eliminate me climbing too many stairs. Andrea immediately found happiness in Denver. She now lived in a town with her two best friends and former roommates from Dallas. It was fun to see Sydney and Jacob fantasize about their bedrooms and the exact location of their swing set. Each vacillated about wall colors. We smiled watching them learn to make independent decisions. Predictably, the kids looked forward to playing in the snow. The dryer climate, cooler temperatures and lower stress from working less were bound to lead me to healthier times. Sydney's middle name, Hope, gave me strength to continue my battle against MS.

Being proactive had paid huge dividends thus far. I knew my work regimen needed to change so I found a new job in Denver. I knew the heat and humidity crushed me physically so we moved away from Houston. I did not like the bedside manner of my neurologist's nurse (carbon copy of Nurse Ratchet from "One Flew Over the Cuckoos Nest") so I switched doctors. I did not like the way one of the ABC drugs made me feel, so I changed medications. The easy decisions were over. Once we moved to Denver it was time to find a new neurologist. I considered the relationship with my doctor a true partnership. Too often people believed every word spoken by their doctor. The doctor told their patient what's wrong or what-to-do and the patient subserviently followed their orders. I wanted a doctor where I could be proactive and suggest where I wanted my care to proceed based on my independent research. I believed a doctor should listen to my needs and provide me alternatives. I wanted to decide what treatment path to take based on perceived risks and potential rewards. Andrea and I researched neurologists on the Internet, through publications and word of mouth. Our efforts pointed us to the Rocky Mountain MS Center. I liked the fact they only treated people afflicted with MS.

After several weeks of phone calls to my insurance company for pre-authorization, I scheduled my first appointment with Dr. Allen Bowling. He had an impressive resume that included the title of Medical Director at the Rocky Mountain MS Center. Dr. Bowling received his undergraduate, M.D., and Ph.D. (pharmacology) degrees at Yale University. He also had expertise in Complementary and Alternative Medicine (CAM). This program focused on herb and vitamin use, diet, and exercise for people with MS.

Working with Dr. Bowling offered me alternatives. He listened to me with an open mind in trying innovative approaches to managing my disease. I needed alternatives because my disease continued to progress. My walking worsened, my legs became tight with spasticity, and I fatigued very early in the day. Once Dr. Bowling heard more about my latest symptoms, he prescribed a combination of interferon shots with methotrexate. This drug showed positive results in making the immune system less active.

MS is widely held to be an autoimmune disease, meaning the immune system is reacting against a component of the normal antigens in the body since these antigens appeared to be foreign. Most researchers believed that damage to myelin, which helped nerve fibers conduct electrical impulses, resulted from an abnormal response by the body's overactive immune system. Normally, the immune system defended the body against viruses or bacteria. In autoimmune diseases like MS, the body attacked its own tissue. I needed to slow down my overactive immune system and methotrexate sounded like a good option.

Dr. Bowling's work with CAM also proved helpful in managing my disease and its symptoms. He suggested changing to a low fat diet, exercising without overheating through water aerobics, and minimizing stress by working less. It did not take me long to consider these ideas. Soon after my first appointment, I implemented all of his recommendations.

It certainly appeared to be a two-way partnership. Through his suggestions, I stayed in front of my disease by continuously making lifestyle adjustments like working less or using a cane to walk safer. Unfortunately my frustration grew large and loud because my walking worsened. Even with a cane, I lost my balance and fell down or tripped on uneven concrete sidewalks. My safety became a real concern. The last thing I wanted or needed was a broken bone. Showering, getting dressed and commuting downtown were hard enough without the inconvenience of a broken arm or leg. The voice in the back of my head challenged the strength of my attitude. "Is it really worth continuing to fight?" I kept falling back on my internal rebuttal that the alternative was unacceptable. Let the mind games begin!

One of my goals in moving to Denver was to slow down and work less. Easier said than done. After accepting my new job and before moving, my future employer asked me to write a business plan for my newly created position. I knew my hours at work should improve. I also thought my travel time would decrease. My business plan included objectives for developing and maintaining insurance sales in three areas: 1) insurance products for mergers and acquisitions; 2) insurance programs for oil and gas companies; and 3) wealth management. I estimated that each of these opportunities should grow through target marketing, networking, and leveraging personal relationships.

My goal was to target M&A opportunities through accountants, attorneys, and investment bankers. Corporate oil and gas programs and wealth management prospects would be secondary objectives. These opportunities should evolve through solving problems using insurance products to facilitate closing deals.

A lot of the networking could be accomplished over the telephone. However, my experience proved in-person meetings were better because you could read people's body language. What I failed to consider was the stress I would encounter establishing this new business division. While my efforts were rewarded through 100% commission compensation, my body paid the price.

The price of my success was measured through my walking. The increase in stress caused my disease to accelerate. I no longer could fly to Houston and back in a day, juggling 3-4 appointments on top of the travel. I worked harder than ever before. While investment banking days proved longer and team driven, my new job was all about me. Unless I picked up the telephone and made the calls, no one would know my insurance solutions existed. The days I spent in the office, I became a calling machine. Most attorneys and investment bankers never returned my calls. I kept calling until they or their assistant agreed to a face-to-face appointment. Several calls abruptly ended with, "Send me something." Those requests gave me an excuse to make a follow-up call. My persistence paid off by closing ten transactions within the first eighteen months of employment.

In addition to phone calls, sales appointments and internal meetings, I also developed relationships with insurance company underwriters. While my company promised me a Client Executive (CE) to negotiate detailed policy language, I needed to understand these unique policies well enough to explain the benefits and considerations of each insurance company program to prospects. Unfortunately, many times CE'S were unavailable and I had to negotiate language myself. That was scary.

My expertise was finding and closing deals, not negotiating words. Insurance companies always wrote their policies to their benefit in anticipation of a lawsuit. Every word had a reason for being on the page. Was an event really covered during a loss? How should I know what words needed to change in order to position the policy language back in my client's favor? Another reason for my trepidation related to no one at work understanding what I worked on every day. Before my employment, nobody used insurance to facilitate M&A transactions. Rather than discussing policy language with internal personnel, I had to ask underwriters the reason for certain wording in their policies. Were they answering my questions truthfully or telling me what I wanted to hear? My concerns bothered me because our competitors had large M&A departments and pre-negotiated policy language that provided greater clarity to questionable terms.

These internal issues caused me great consternation because corporate M&A activity significantly slowed in 2000 due to rising interest rates and the impending recession. Higher rates meant the cost of borrowing money to finance transactions might eliminate positive deal economics. While 100% commission compensation sounded good in an active M&A environment, I feared my failure in a slower, less active transactional landscape. A lesser amount of transactions meant a lower level of commissions. Without a salary to backstop the slowdown, my anxiety grew. I could not and would not let my financial failure touch the lives of Andrea and the kids.

I needed to find a job with similar responsibilities that offered a stable salary plus some bonus potential tied to my transactional success. The phone was my friend so I cold-called the office manager of Marsh USA, the world's largest risk manager and insurance broker with an office in Denver. My first call rolled to his voice mail. I decided to leave him a message. "We've never met and you probably don't know me, but I have a skill set that could benefit your office. Please call me so we can discuss further." Soon after, I received a return phone call from his Sales Manager. We arranged a breakfast meeting for later in the week.

Before the interview I vacillated on whether or not to use my cane. My balance had worsened. I knew I needed the cane to keep me from falling on my face. But I was frightened by the first perception. Engineering school taught me you never get a second chance to make a good first impression. I feared the Sales Manager would think, "He stumbles with a cane. What's wrong with him? Will he only get worse and be a liability to my company?" I did not want to explain my disease and detract from the purpose of the meeting. I also did not have a good understanding of employee rights through the Americans with Disabilities Act of 1990 (ADA). While ADA had 10 years of history, my paranoia overtook what a reasonable person should think. I only considered the worse case scenario - not being hired for the job. I needed this job. My paranoia caused me to go to the interview without the cane. I arrived early to the meeting, stumbled up the stairs to the restaurant and secured a table so the Sales Manager would not see me grabbing chairs for balance while I waddled to my seat.

Interviews for me were the equivalent of a sales call. My resume only offered a snapshot of me at a point in time. It did not capture my personality. I looked forward to this meeting since it gave me the opportunity to show my people skills and how I could add value to her team.

The Sales Manager informed me her company wanted a local salesperson that would specialize in environmental insurance. I knew I could offer her local deal facilitation with this product. More than 50% of the transactions I completed to date used environmental insurance in lieu of indemnification language in purchase and sales contracts. I also offered another selling point. I recently authored an article on the benefits of using environmental insurance in M&A transactions. The previous week, my article was accepted for publication in the Oil and Gas Investor magazine. This magazine was the gold standard publication for senior oil and gas executives, research analysts and finance professionals. Being a published author on environmental insurance provided me with instant credibility on the subject.

With confidence I said, "You need to look no further. The position you described sounds exactly what I want. What are the next steps in your process?"

"I would like you to meet with our office manager and one of the top environmental insurance experts in the country. Lucky for us she lives and works in Denver. She specializes in BRAC's - Base Realignments and Closures. Most of these base closures have considerable environmental contamination from years of fuel seepage and spills that leached into the groundwater. Since she travels a lot, it might take a few weeks to find an available lunch date. I like your background and selling skills. We need to make this work."

My fourteen years of sales experience taught me how to read people's body language and buying signals. The Sales Manager and I connected with similar aggressive, honest and deliberate mentalities. I felt really good about this opportunity. We both drank several cups of coffee during our meeting. While she and I both needed to use the restroom, I decided to wait for her at our table. If I walked too fast because of the urgency, I might trip and fall. My paranoia forced me to wait. When she returned, I stood up and braced myself with both hands on the table. Once I found my balance and equilibrium, I walked one step behind her to hide my unstable gait. This also blocked her from seeing me grab each chair for stability while we walked outside. Luckily, the restaurant had handrails on both sides of the steps leading down to the parking lot. While I held on to both rails, I thanked Kathy for breakfast and told her I looked forward to hearing from her. Thankfully, she never noticed my inability to walk in a straight line.

Once again, I successfully landed at a new employer. Work proved to be overwhelming yet very satisfying because I worked on bigger and more complex opportunities. I did not encounter any significant health events for about a year. Was my disease in remission? Not likely. My walking continued to worsen. My cane became the crutch necessary to walk safely. Numerous times my right foot found the uneven sidewalk surface before me flying through the air horizontally. My cane launched like a flying projectile. From that point forward, I labeled these episodes "eating concrete".

What would people think of me? Using my cane full time caused me to face reality and recognize I could no longer claim to be bullet proof and immortal. Investment banking taught me to lead with power and outwardly show my strength. Senior management wanted investment bankers who had confidence and knowledge of their business. They did not have patience for someone being cautious or tentative. Weakness, or perceived weakness, was unacceptable. Unfortunately I no longer had a choice. I could not walk without my cane.

My conclusion, after much internal debate, was to be honest with my employer and myself. I created so much stress worrying about this decision. At dinner one night Sydney asked me, "Dad, what are you looking at?" My eyes lost focus while I gazed outside towards the foothills with too much on my mind. My secret haunted me through many restless and sleepless nights. No one knew about my disease other than my family and close friends. That was up to and including the time I wobbled into my boss's office – with my cane.

Kathy appeared to be deep in conversation on the telephone. She pointed towards one of her high back chairs opposite her desk and whispered for me to sit down. She finished the call, hung up the phone and smiled at me. "Mr. Sloan, what can I do for you? You are having a great year so far. Whatever you're doing, keep charging! What's on your mind?"

I took a deep breath and slowly blew out. My heart raced like it did on my first date or first kiss. "This won't take long. I know you are extremely busy. You probably noticed me walking in here with a cane. You deserve to know why. In October 1998, I was diagnosed with MS. Recently I started using a cane to help me walk safely. I'm not asking for any accommodations from Marsh. I believe in full disclosure and wanted you and our office personnel to know I am living with MS."

Kathy's face showed compassion and real concern. "OK. You are very thoughtful to tell me. My husband and I have several close friends with MS. I know you are a very independent person. Just let me know if and when we can do anything, and I really mean that, to make your life easier."

Once we honestly discussed my health, I felt liberated. Now my employer knew about my disease. On one hand, honesty made life easier at work. On the other hand, my outside work in sales became harder. I continued to hide my illness from most clients and prospects. While I wanted to let everyone know, I once again had a perception problem. On the telephone, no one could tell. At meetings, I looked at people as they looked at me. What are they thinking? Can they tell? Am I wasting my time? My secret tormented me to the point of distraction. How could I sell my company and me with so much anguish?

One night the issue climaxed. I hosted a client and close friend at a hockey game at the Pepsi Center. I drove my car to the game and we walked, without my cane, from the parking lot to our seats. We walked in between cars so I could use them for balance. Then we reached an open space between the cars and the front doors. My fatigue and unsteadiness increased. I needed to slow down because sweat poured from my forehead. The walk seemed like several miles. In reality the distance was only 200 yards. While Rick knew I had MS, he did not know I walked with a cane. About 50 feet from the entrance, Rick stopped me. "David, what's wrong? You seem to have problems walking." I could not lie to him. I told Rick I began using a cane at work to make walking safer. Then he let me have a piece of his mind. "You need to get over it. I pay for the use of your mind, not your legs. If you need to use a cane who cares? Not me." From that day forward I let my guard down and decided full disclosure made sense.

It was a silly mind game being afraid to let people know about my disease and using a cane. Once again I felt relieved. I thought people would not want to conduct business with me because of my disability. Nothing could be further from the truth. People's curiosity prompted questions about my disease like when I received my diagnosis or what treatments I used to slow the progression. Their compassion for me regarding my willingness to fight gave me strength. I did not give people enough credit for the size of their hearts. People really did care about me. People really did care about other people. Everything I knew about power and appearance proved to be only part of the story. MS did not make me who I am. My attitude, my love for life, and my hope for better days ahead defined who I am. Honesty with others improved how I felt about me. It shattered my perceptions of other people. My new business production actually increased and had nothing to do with my false perceptions. So I opened up to everyone – everyone except my mom.

When should I tell her? What should I tell her? My dad and I had several conversations about the subject. He told me, "It's not worth burdening her. The news will make you feel better but not her. Why tell her so she can beat herself up every day lying in her nursing home bed thinking it's her fault?" I was tired of living the lie. I told my dad it wasn't *if* I would tell her, but *when* I would tell her. I was eager to tell her, especially after feeling so much better once I made the disclosure at work. Up to this moment, whenever we traveled to St. Louis to see my mom and dad, I would leave my cane outside of her room and hold Andrea's hand while I stumbled to her bedside.

We made our next trip during the summer of 2002. Once we reached St. Louis, we stopped at the nursing home. The TV blared loudly in the background in her room. The Post Dispatch newspaper lay all over her bed. Her Walgreen's magnifying glasses were halfway down her nose while she played her daily Jumble puzzle. I looked at Andrea and asked, "How do they speak to each other with the TV so loud?" Maybe that was the point after 45 years of marriage.

My mom and dad greeted us with excitement in their voices. My mom's eyes lit up when Sydney and Jacob entered her room. While she liked to see Andrea and me, she lived to see her grandkids. On our long walk to my mom's room, I told Andrea I wanted to spend some time alone with her the following morning. The time had come to stop living the lie.

The next morning I drove myself back to the nursing home. I stumbled through the hallways with my cane. The 100 yards seemed like 10 miles. My stomach tightened with nerves. The sweat beaded on my forehead. I kept pleading with myself to slow down and be safe. The walk tired me out on the journey to her room. I panted until I reached my final destination. This time I did not leave my cane outside her room leaning against the doorjamb. Immediately she slammed me with questions. "David, what gives me the pleasure of your company so early in the morning? Did you watch the baseball Cardinals play last night after you left? Why are you using a cane?"

It was my turn to do the talking. "Mom, I've wanted to tell you something for a long time. The reason I use a cane relates to my health. Almost four years ago I was diagnosed with MS. The disease didn't affect my walking for several years. I started using the cane full time last year." I paused and looked at my mom to check her reaction through her facial expressions. She had no tears.

My inward fears of telling her vanished. There was a long pause while she considered her response. I kept staring at her eyes waiting for the waterfall of tears streaming down her face. They never came. Her temporary silence increased my anxiety. She stared out the window for several seconds before looking back at me.

"Really. What type of MS do you have? I have chronic progressive. Did you know you have two cousins who also have MS? How long did it take your doctor to figure it out?"

Listening to her questions that came without emotion reinforced my belief in her incredible compassion. I breathed in deep and let out a forceful sigh of relief. My mom was an amazing woman.

We talked until lunchtime. Her room became hot from the sunshine and our heavy conversation. I walked with my cane over to her air conditioner and turned the temperature down and the blower on high. She never led me to believe she blamed herself for my disease. Only time away from her would tell me how the news truly affected her. Her questions came more out of curiosity. While I always jested calling myself the "poor neglected middle child", my mom always considered me the chosen one. We could talk about anything and anyone. I was the great negotiator between my brother Mike, who was four years older and my brother Steve, who was five years younger. The age difference between Mike and Steve created a great divide of common interests. I bridged the gap to find common ground.

What a wonderful feeling to have this burden I carried inside me vanish through honesty. In a matter of hours, releasing the tremendous burden of living this lie had lifted my spirits. My smiles became real again. "Mom, now that you know, how do you feel about my news? Be honest with me."

"David, I love you – regardless of your disease. I wish you had told me sooner. I hope you will eventually realize MS is something you have, not who you are. Look at me. Do I wish my life turned out differently? Sure I do." My mom talked so clearly with strong conviction in her voice. "Your attitude should help you persevere through many rough days in front of you. You and I are so much alike. Always remember to focus on the things you can still accomplish. Don't waste time dwelling on the things you can't do anymore. It's a waste of time. Believe me, I know." This woman gave me strength and empowered me through every word from her mouth.

I stood up, walked over to her bed, and gave my mom a big hug and kiss. Her words resonated throughout my body. If she can do it, so can I. What a wonderful role model.

Now my mom and I had something in common. It felt so good to talk openly with her. Several times on the telephone she asked me how the disease affected my ability to work and be a good father. We had something that tied us together. I had no regrets telling her. Once again, I felt liberated to stop living another lie.

6

SAFETY IS MORE IMPORTANT

Every day proved to be an adventure. I constantly had to change my lifestyle. Internally I complained to myself and cussed a lot. Every time I fell caused more frustration. No one, except Andrea, knew of my frustration since I always "walked" around with a smile on my face but this disease really sucked. While my walking worsened with the progression of my disease, my attitude never wavered. My mom always used an expression that gained new meaning with me. "David, one day at a time." Adaptation became my middle name.

I wanted to do everything humanly possible to keep walking. It scared me to think about using a wheelchair. In my mind, walking with a cane had a different connotation than wheeling around in a wheelchair. Would people think I had given up? Would I be one step closer to a nursing home? How long before I'm bedridden? My mind raced wildly, consumed with the fear of wheelchairs. I connected dots that did not exist.

So I kept trying ways to keep me upright. One of my problems related to my right foot dragging. The lack of strength in my hip flexors caused my right foot to drag. It inevitably caught on uneven surfaces like raised sidewalks. The palms of my hands paid the price when they landed on the sidewalk first. Thankfully strangers helped pick me up. It took all of my strength to get on my hands and knees. I'd pause, breathing heavily, before attempting to stand upright. Several deep breaths later, I grabbed my cane from the kind stranger and resumed my walk. Each step forced me to look down at my feet and watch for the next break in the sidewalk. I dreaded explaining the reasons for my new skinned knee or elbow to Andrea or the kids. Sydney or Jacob would always ask, "Where did that boo-boo come from?" I didn't want to trouble Andrea or admit to myself I had worsened.

Faced with another problem to solve, I discussed my concrete consumption with my neurologist. Dr. Bowling prescribed an ankle foot orthotic, or AFO. An AFO provides ankle support and controls the ankle through a hinge mechanism that helps lift the foot with each step. The device molded to my foot and calf and slipped inside my shoe on top of my sock. While it definitely helped minimize falling, my regular work shoes were too narrow. I had to order triple E custom shoes to accommodate the AFO in my right shoe. All it took was money.

Thankfully, Marsh offered excellent healthcare coverage for employees and their families. Even though I saw a number of doctors, I only had to pay a $20 or $40 co-pay for each visit. While my injectable ABC interferon medication cost approximately $15,000 per year, I paid $40 for a three-month supply through our mail-order pharmacy.

While I lived with a chronic disease, it took four years of fighting the symptoms before I admitted this reality to myself. My battle had only just begun. The one constant factor throughout my fight was my positive attitude. I would not let MS get the best of me. Yes, I fought the inconveniences thrown in my face. But I woke up every day contemplating what else I could do to make life easier.

The AFO definitely helped minimize my falling since it reduced my problems with foot drop. It did not, however, eliminate my stumbling or crashing into door jams. Andrea and the kids always knew when I fell because my falls were loud. My body paid the price through cuts and deep bruises.

One reason for my falls related to spasticity. My leg muscles continuously contracted to the point of them not bending. I felt like a toy soldier marching with straight legs. Only my walking never occurred in a straight line. Spasticity is usually caused by damage to the portion of the brain or spinal cord that controls voluntary movement. My symptoms included increased muscle tone, clonus (a series of rapid muscle contractions), exaggerated deep tendon reflexes and muscle spasms.

Dr. Bowling prescribed oral Baclofen. These pills provided relief assuming I took them religiously every four hours. After several months of increasing the dose, he also suggested me taking a second spasticity medicine called Zanoflex. The combination of these drugs worked great, with one exception. The Zanoflex caused me to be very drowsy.

The issue climaxed one morning while driving to work. I had just driven past Mississippi Street on Santa Fe on my way to I-25. Although it was only 7:30 am, I could not keep my eyes open. I nodded off. Luckily I caught myself before hitting anyone or anything with my car. While I needed the drugs to minimize the spasticity, the side effects proved intolerable. Something had to change.

Once again the Rocky Mountain MS Center delivered timely resources. Every Wednesday the Center offered a Spasticity Clinic. Two doctors and a physical therapist from the Heuga Center evaluated my spasticity. They checked the tightness of my arms and legs, and filmed me walking up and down the hallway. The team caucused and provided me their recommendations.

The following week I returned for treatment. Much to my surprise, they wanted to inject botox into my calf muscles. I jested with Dr. Seeberger that regardless of the success of the injections, at least my calves would be wrinkle free! Unfortunately, after two weeks of injections I did not feel any improvement. What should I do now? I had to figure out someway to alleviate my spasticity problems without compromising my safety. While my frustration increased, I quickly learned that doctors did not measure success in terms of black or white. There were many shades of gray. Trial and error proved to be the only way to find a solution.

When I first visited the Spasticity Clinic, Dr. Karen Theriot mentioned a few alternatives for me to consider. Unfortunately, her list was short. Since Botox did not provide me any relief from my stiffness, a surgical option became my best choice. She suggested an intrathecal baclofen pump.

A baclofen pump delivers medication directly into an area of the spine called the intrathecal space. The intrathecal space contains the cerebrospinal fluid -- the fluid surrounding the spinal cord and nerve roots. The intrathecal baclofen pump continuously delivers the drug right to the target site in the spinal cord. Since the medication is not swallowed and digested before crossing the blood brain barrier, only tiny doses are required to be effective. Therefore, side effects are minimal. I wouldn't have to monitor my watch and determine when I should take the next dose of oral medication. Many times I forgot to take a dose or found myself caught in a meeting without my pills. After these blunders, I became a stiff legged toy soldier again. By eliminating the drug passing through my digestive system, there would be no lag in receiving relief from my symptoms. I liked the sound of this delivery system already.

The intrathecal baclofen pump system consisted of a catheter (a small, flexible tube) and a pump. The pump - a round metal disc, about one inch thick and three inches in diameter – would be surgically placed under the skin of the abdomen near the waistline. Made of titanium, it looked like a metal hockey puck. The pump stored and released prescribed amounts of medicine through the catheter. With a programmable pump, a tiny motor moved the medication from the pump reservoir through the catheter. Using an external programmer, doctors could make adjustments in the dose, rate, and timing of the medication.

People with pumps must return to their doctor's office for pump refills and medication adjustments every 30-90 days. The pump is taken out and replaced at the end of the battery's life span, usually five to seven years.

Sydney and Jacob loved asking me how many doctors I had. No wonder. Their astute young minds focused on my endless doctor appointments. Every week another doctor wanted to see me. When would my boss finally question my time away from work? Luckily my sales position afforded me the luxury of controlling my schedule. Assuming I met or exceeded my production goals, my time away would not be an issue. While I tried to see doctors before or after outside sales calls, I constantly juggled between my job responsibilities and health care providers.

In order to determine if I proved to be a good candidate for a pump, I checked into Swedish Medical Center for a day procedure. I had to stop taking all spasticity medications twelve hours before the test. I felt so stiff without them. Dr. Theriot injected liquid baclofen into the intrathecal space of my spinal cord, very similar to a spinal tap. She videotaped me walking with my cane at one, three, and five hours intervals after the procedure and compared those results with my walking at the Spasticity Clinic the previous week. My results showed a favorable response to the medication leading to surgically implanting the pump.

The following week I met with Dr. Scott Falci, the Neurosurgeon selected by Dr. Theriot to implant my pump. The same day I also completed pre-op blood work. Dr. Falci scheduled the surgery on the next Thursday at 4:00 pm. He instructed me to discontinue all food consumption by 7:00 pm the night before surgery and to check into the hospital at 2:00 pm. I was so eager to solve another nagging problem that plagued my ability to live life "normally".

The day of surgery, my phone rang around 10:00 am. The receptionist at Dr. Falci's office informed me he just entered an emergency spinal cord surgery and my procedure might be delayed several hours. She would call me after she knew when I should arrive at the hospital. At 4:00 pm, I got tired of watching the phone and called his office. I was beyond starved. I wanted answers. "When should I check into the hospital?" She still had no answer for me other than, "We may need to reschedule your surgery." I jumped back and told her, "I've gone an entire day without eating. I'm starved. This needs to happen today."

At 7:00 pm, Dr. Falci's surgical assistant called me and asked if I still wanted the surgery today. "Absolutely." She told me to check-in at 10:00 pm. Andrea looked at me like I was crazy. "How are we going to do this with the kids? I can't stay with you. They need to go to bed." I told her I could drive myself to the hospital. That was unacceptable to her. She told me she would drive me with the kids and stay through check-in. "Once they take you to pre-op, I'll ask the nurse to call me when they finish."

They wheeled me into the operating room at 11:00 pm. I felt uneasy. With my surgery scheduled so late, would Dr. Falci still be able to perform without mistakes? I hoped he had good malpractice insurance. After he entered the operating room I asked him, "Doc, how do you feel? You're not going to fall asleep on me are you?" He laughed. "Compared to my last procedure, this will be a cake walk. Don't worry about anything, we'll take really good care of you."

Dr. Falci's assistant Charlotte called Andrea around 2:00 am. "Everything went fine. He'll be in his room in about an hour after he wakes up from the anesthesia. I'll come by his room and check on him sometime in the early afternoon."

When I first considered whether or not to have the surgery to install the pump, I only thought of the positive implications. No more oral spasticity medication, less stiffness, better sleep because of reduced overnight spasms and the ability to increase the dose in small amounts when necessary. I did not, however, think about how my body would react to the surgery. Dr. Theriot originally told me I would be in and out of the hospital in three days. But several factors caused me to stay in the hospital for seven days.

Most people bounced back and felt better after a minor surgical procedure. I did not. The trauma and pain from the incisions in my back and abdomen created problems with my legs. It took several days of changing the pump dose so I could place enough weight on my legs so I did not tip over. I also learned that too much of the medicine caused my legs to feel rubbery to the point of not holding my bodyweight. Once I had the proper dose, I still needed to relearn how to walk using a walker. This was a major stress factor for me because before to the surgery, I walked with a cane. I lay in my hospital bed for hours contemplating the possibilities. Did the negatives outweigh the benefits for installing the pump? Did the quality of my life really improve? Only through the passage of time would I know the answers to these questions.

One issue became very clear. I could no longer walk long distances safely with my cane. It only took a few weeks after my surgery to reach this painful conclusion. My spasticity improved with the pump, but I started falling more often because my disease continued to progress. A bad fall might jar the catheter loose from the pump. Please, not another surgery. This disease caused me to constantly shake my head in disbelief of my proactive decisions. I wanted to win my battle with MS and safely walk again without assistance. Was I being unrealistic? All I needed were new legs.

My downward spiral from setbacks melted my positive attitude. I questioned all of my previous decisions. Why did I constantly need to look for ways to make life easier? When would I feel better? What's the point of fighting back when I kept getting worse? Every time I had these thoughts, I fought back my tears of despair. I yearned for my life back before the diagnosis of MS.

I missed taking long walks with Andrea hand-in-hand. Every night after dinner the trees swayed back-and-forth with the hot summertime Dallas winds blowing through our hair. We walked and talked about our dreams of having kids and raising them with a mid-West, common sense value system. We liked to fantasize about traveling together. Where do we want go on vacation to scuba dive and lay on the beach? What about New Orleans for Jazz Fest? Live music and Cajun food wet our appetites for next year's festival. I missed climbing stairs with Sydney and Jacob up to their bedrooms. After sitting on the carpet, both kids sat in my lap. We read several books together before bedtime. I cherished this time with them. After finishing every night, I tucked them into their separate beds and told them how much I loved them.

Enough nonsense. I had to stop feeling sorry for myself. Once again, the voice in the back of my head provided me answers. "Are you serious? How dare you question your aggressive, proactive and unbelievably positive attitude. Healthy friends, family and colleagues admire your approach to life. Stop falling down the wormhole of what is bad and getting worse in your life. Concentrate on the good things: loving wife and kids, great friends and undeniable fortitude. Get over yourself. Move on."

When I opened my eyes, the wormhole looked wide, endlessly deep and very black. Rather than tumbling downward and out of control, I smiled and laughed at myself. How could I ever give up? Not now, not ever. I woke up from my living nightmare and returned to solving problems. For example, Dr. Theriot prescribed an electric scooter for traveling long distances instead of walking from my car to my office. She wanted me to continue walking with my cane, but over shorter distances. I waited several weeks for my insurance company to approve this piece of durable medical equipment. The approval came with another dose of reality. How would I transport the scooter from home to work? The scooter weighed nearly 175 pounds. How would I lift the scooter into and out of my car?

I swallowed hard. I had to sell my Mercedes and find a SUV that could hold the scooter in the rear storage area. I loved my Mercedes. This was my dream car – Silver E-320, four doors, monster stereo system, sunroof, AWD, and very, very fast. The car gave me confidence. The car brought me back to the fast lane of my power driven investment banking days before my MS diagnosis. And now I had to make another personal sacrifice in the name of safety. When would this stop?

While I enjoyed negotiating the purchase of new cars, I hated selling vehicles. I had no control on the sell side. People had to answer my ad. Hopefully someone would call. When someone called, they always wanted a really good deal. The most likely scenario meant losing a lot of money selling the Mercedes in the name of safety. Purchasing and installing the lift cost several thousand dollars in cash. Sure we could claim the expenses as miscellaneous medical expenses – assuming the costs exceeded 7.5% of our adjusted gross income. All I could do was stare at the floor, shake my head, blow air through my nostrils and press my lips tightly together. Damn it! These years were supposed to be the most productive years of my life. Instead, I walked away from my dream job and watched my body self-destruct. I felt so powerless and out of control.

Unfortunately, no one called for my Mercedes. But I could not wait for the car to sell before buying a car for the scooter. Another mission. This problem had to be solved quickly. I needed to buy a new car before the delivery of the scooter. Andrea watched me in disbelief. She saw me focus on solving a singular task with a very specific timeline. I reverted back to my M&A days in deal mode. My mind had tunnel vision towards completing this task.

"David, where are you going? How many nights will this go on? You've been going to car dealers every night after work."

I spent hours on the phone and visited eight car dealers to measure the height, width and depth of several SUV rear compartments. I had very specific dimensions of the scooter and needed vertical clearance for lifting the scooter into and out of this space. I finally settled on a Honda Pilot.

On the same date of delivery, I drove my new car to a company that specialized in adaptive equipment for automobiles. Andrea followed me with the scooter in the back of her minivan. They installed a Bruno Curb-Sider Lift in the rear storage space of my car and connected a docking device to the scooter. A hand-held keypad lifted the scooter up while I guided it out of my car and onto the ground.

Another problem solved. Yee-hah! I still had the ability to focus on an objective, identify the issues, develop alternatives, and solve the problem. Engineering school taught me well. While I had no way to anticipate what lie ahead of me, I braced myself for the next crisis yet to confront me. Good or bad, I knew it was out there.

7

WELCOME TO BRAZIL

My health continued to regress despite changes in treatment medications, increases in the amount of exercise and adjustments to my diet. Yes, I felt better living in the drier climate of Denver compared to Houston, but I needed to be honest with myself. My walking was at the point of needing an electric scooter to be mobile and safe during the day. How else could I get around to make sales calls? My biggest fear was being bed-ridden in a nursing home like my mom. That was unacceptable to me. It was devastating to see my body deteriorate. I fell almost every day and my arms lost power throughout the day. Desperation started to overtake my normally positive attitude. While driving home through 45 minutes of traffic, my mind wandered away from the road. What do I do now? None of the medications are slowing the progression of my disease. There must be something or someone to feed my desperate attempts to keep trying.

A phone call from my cousin Betsy changed my thinking. She had just returned from her trip to a town in Brazil called Abadiânia. In this town, a man named João de Deus (John or God) healed people. "David, before I went I was extremely skeptical. After spending two weeks in Brazil I'm convinced you have to go," she told me with strong conviction. She piqued my interest. I needed to meet this man and experience a different type of healing – spiritual healing. Until now, I had demanded empirical evidence before trying new medications. My engineering background made me crave numbers to make educated decisions. Betsy had opened a crack in my rigid belief system. She introduced vocabulary and mystical views toward life. Within minutes of her call, I already felt beyond my comfort zone. While I contemplated our discussion, I reflected back to my mantra of always wanting to touch the outside edge of possible therapies. Why not go to Brazil? What stopped me? The fear of the unknown caused me to shift my reality towards something new. Something intangible.

Who was this John of God person? My research revealed him to be a medium dedicated to healing others. João de Teixeira de Faria was born in 1942 in Goiás, Brazil. From a very young age, he was clairvoyant and able to predict many events before they occurred. One story described him saving both his mother and him by knowing to leave his village before a destructive rainstorm with flooding that seemed to come out of nowhere.

This man had no formal training. He left school after the second grade. His life changed dramatically when he was sixteen. As described on healingquests.com, "He had been traveling from town to town looking for work, without much success, and was exhausted and hungry. He stopped near a stream and had a vision of a beautiful woman who told him he was needed in a nearby church in the town of Campo Grande (Matto Grosso) and to go there because people were waiting for him. He later realized the woman was the spirit of St. Rita of Cassia. He followed her directions, and as she had predicted, was welcomed at the church. That was all he remembered until hours later when he awakened and was told that King Solomon had incorporated in him and healed many people. He protested that hunger and exhaustion had made him faint, but the many witnesses to the healing miracles left no doubt that he had been the medium for extraordinary healing from the spiritual plane.

An intense period of instruction and guidance ensued over the next several weeks. João was directed to dedicate his life to healing others and never to accept payment for this work, a guideline he follows to this day. For eight years, John of God traveled the region finding work when he could in order to eat, devoting his remaining time to healing others. They came to him by the hundreds as word of his abilities spread. It was necessary not to stay in any one place for too long. Though he never profited from his mediumship, the local religious and medical authorities were threatened and set the police on him. Many times he was arrested, beaten and jailed.

When he could no longer take this persecution he obtained a job as a tailor for the military in Brasilia. In exchange for safety he performed healings on the military personnel and their families. This nine-year period ended when the spirit entities told him that his work must be made available to many instead of just the privileged few. He was guided to Abadiânia and established a center there in a small building off the main highway. In 1978 he moved the center to its present location, creating Casa de Dom Inácio."

For 43 years, João's channeled over 30 spirit entities for thousands of people every week. The healing entities that work through John of God are spirits of deceased doctors, surgeons, masters and saints. As a full trance medium, spirits incorporate into his physical body so completely that John of God never recalls the work performed through him. Occasionally, spirits make their identities known. More often, John of God's assistants identify which spirit worked through him on different days. The most prevalent spirit among them is St. Ignatius Loyola. The Casa was named after this spirit. Other spirits include Oswaldo Cruz, a famous doctor in Brazil over 100 years ago. This man eradicated yellow fever and was a key figure in the founding of Brasilia. Another includes Dr. Augusto de Almeida, a surgeon and spiritual master who performs many of the surgeries.

My initial reaction to this information was disbelief. I could only be proven wrong by seeing this man with my own eyes. What was my cousin getting me into? What does it mean to incorporate into someone's body? I quickly realized I was entering a new phase in my healing journey that was beyond comprehension. The voice inside my head reminded me why I had to go: "You have to keep an open mind or traveling 5,300 miles will be a waste of time. You know you need a miracle to walk again and John of God is going to help."

Once I made the decision, there was much work to do. My cousin recommended traveling to Abadiânia with a guide since I would be traveling alone and needing an interpreter once in Brazil. Betsy suggested a woman named Josie RavenWing. She believed Josie could simplify my travel experience. This woman had begun leading healing journeys to Brazil and The Casa de Dom Inácio facility in 1998. She taught herself Portuguese and studied shamanic and other spiritual paths since the late '60s. Josie was quite informative about the necessary paperwork leading up to our trip in August. For example, I needed a Brazilian visa attached to my passport. While I was reluctant to mail my passport to the Houston-based Brazilian consulate, I followed Josie's advice so my passport and visa would arrive before our trip. She also suggested a travel agent who could arrange my flights to coincide with her plane leaving from Miami to Sao Paulo in Brazil. Josie simplified an overwhelming journey.

After completing the paperwork and travel plans, Betsy suggested reviewing the Friends of The Casa de Dom Inácio website (http://www.friendsofthecasa.org). On the website Betsy noticed that some guides offered to take your photo in front of João for distant healing. If João marked an "X" on your photo it meant that you were ready to receive a spiritual operation when you arrived. What did that mean? While skeptical and somewhat untrusting, I picked a woman from the website based in New York City. I sent my picture and money for a prescription of herbs made from passionflowers.

Sending money to a stranger for herbs violated my conservative value system. Were they legal? What did they do? A phone call with Betsy answered my questions. She told me the herbs had no medicinal value. The power of the supplement was in the energy placed in my specific herbs by the entity. They were for me and nobody else. All of this new terminology was both refreshing and scary.

Jumping into the world of spirituality opened my mind to new words, non-empirically based events, and new hope for walking again. Yet, how could I be so accepting? Why take pills that have no medicinal value? Did this man really pick herbs for me based on my letter sent to a total stranger? This whole journey reeked of a scam. What was I getting myself into? What made me so willing to believe this man named John of God who lived in a foreign land? My understanding of healing and spirituality meant nothing compared to what I was about to experience.

Josie suggested completing some homework to bring with me to Brazil. She asked me to write a letter to João that described my story in greater detail and what I expected to accomplish. The letter to João would be left at the Prayer Triangle in the main meeting area of The Casa. She also wanted me to develop a short list of goals during my stay in Brazil. Below is the letter I wrote:

August 14, 2004

Dear João (John of God):

My name is David Mark Sloan. In October 1998, I was diagnosed with multiple sclerosis. In order to reduce symptoms and slow the progression of the disease, I resigned from my job while living in Houston, Texas. My family and I moved to Denver, Colorado where we currently live. The climate is much better (drier) for my disease but my condition continues to worsen. I can no longer walk without the assistance of a cane. I use an electric scooter for mobility so I don't fall. At home I use a walker for stability.

My cousin recently visited your facility in April 2004. Based on her experiences, I am traveling to Abadiânia on August 15-28 to meet you and begin the spiritual journey of healing. Science and medicine have not helped my medical condition. Since my diagnosis in 1998 I continue to worsen even though I take a very aggressive healing approach using many medications. Now it is time for me to try a new approach. Now it is time to experience spiritual healing with your assistance.

I recognize my journey may take a long time and require several visits with you. I have patience and want to use your guidance and healing powers to accomplish the following goals:

1. *I want to be healthy with no symptoms from multiple sclerosis;*

2. *I want to walk safely again without the assistance of a cane or my electric scooter;*

3. *I want to receive energy such that I am no longer constrained in what I eat (I currently have an intolerance to foods with gluten);*

4. *I want to be able to take long walks with my wife while holding hands with her;*

5. *I want to be able to travel with my family without concern of any disabilities I currently experience;*

6. *I want to be able to be outside in the sunshine without worrying about weakening symptoms created from this exposure;*

7. *I want to give back to my community such that I can help others overcome their challenges;*

8. *I want to continue my belief in Positive Mental Attitude since I know a person's attitude helps provide positive energy.*

I want to take this opportunity in advance of meeting you to express my gratitude for what you accomplish by helping others.

Thank you for being a good person who wants to help others. I look forward to meeting you and feeling your energy. Please share your energy and light to manifest my goals.

With much love,

David Mark Sloan

This letter was the most open and honest I had been with myself and written to a total stranger. Something was happening to me before ever leaving for Brazil. Josie wanted me to develop goals so I could visualize them during each of our sessions in the current room. They needed to be simple, positive goals without many words. Rather than saying "I don't want to be afflicted with MS any longer," the goal should be "remove MS from my body." She continued on the phone, "All goals should be directed towards the spirit entities and their ability to heal. Only one spirit incorporated into João at any moment. Many other spirits heal people at The Casa even though you can't see them."

My mind struggled to comprehend spiritual healing and spirit entities. The only way for me to picture these entities was seeing ghosts flying around the facility healing people. I easily summarized my goals after writing my letter to João: 1) remove MS from my body, 2) walk unassisted, 3) heal my gluten intolerance, and 4) enjoy sunshine without MS symptoms. With my homework now complete, it was time to leave Denver on my mind-expanding adventure.

We left our house for the Denver airport early Sunday morning. While the sun broke through the low-lying clouds, I stared at myself in the passenger side mirror. My bright blue Hawaiian shirt woke me up better than two cups of coffee. On the drive to the airport, the kids kept asking me, "What are you going to do in Brazil?" They could not understand me seeing a spiritual healer. I had a hard time explaining my daily activities in Brazil because I really didn't know. The only thing I could tell them was, "Dad is going to feel better when you see me in two weeks." I looked over at Andrea driving my car. She had a very serious look on her face. She was very concerned about me traveling by myself on three different airplanes more than 5,300 miles. Traveling on any plane was hard for me. I had to drive my scooter to the door of the airplane and airline personnel would strap me into an "aisle chair" that wheeled me to my seat. "How are you going to get to the bathroom from your seat?" was one of Andrea's many questions. She had every reason to be concerned. I was traveling alone in a foreign country where most people did not speak English. But I was so excited the logistical issues seemed inconsequential.

My plane arrived in Miami. From the airplane, I saw palm trees blowing back and forth in the afternoon heat. Before we landed, a wave of sadness overcame me. I desperately wanted to walk again. The fear of the unknown and leaving my family for two weeks brought tears to my eyes. I kept saying to myself, "I cannot believe I'm really doing this. What are my co-workers saying about me?" It didn't matter. I was at the point of doing anything to feel better and walk again. My layover between flights was more than five hours. In the Miami airport, I got a sense for the language barrier I was about to experience. There were so many different languages being spoken. It was similar to New York City with its many cultures and languages. I always got mad at home when hearing foreigners speaking in their native language when they should be speaking English. How hypocritical of me for not learning to speak some Portuguese. I was lazy since Josie spoke their language.

The humidity in the air at the Miami airport was stifling. My body felt heavy and stiff. I sweated uncontrollably like when I lived in Houston. We finally took off for São Paolo. Once away from Miami at 40,000 feet I felt better. Feeling better was a very good omen. Hope lifted my spirits. I closed my eyes and saw myself smiling. Positive thoughts once again filled my mind.

We landed in São Paolo. It was dark outside. People kept bumping into me as they scrambled to leave the airplane. I felt so tired. Brazil was 3 hours ahead of Denver so my body clock thought we arrived in the middle of the night. Unfortunately I did not sleep on the airplane. There were too many distractions – babies crying and people in adjacent rows needing to use the bathroom. My seat would pull back and forth as people stood up. Going to the bathroom mid-flight proved to be more challenging than Andrea feared. It was not easy but I managed to use each seat for leverage while I slowly made my way to the bathroom. I'm sure I startled and woke up many people after passing their seats, but at least I didn't fall. My biggest concerns and fears were whether my scooter was on the airplane and whether it would arrive at all.

I was always the last person off an airplane. "Please let my scooter make it," I pleaded to myself. It took more than 30 minutes to bring the scooter to me, but it had made the journey unscathed across the ocean. "One more plane and I'm done for two weeks," I exhaled with excitement. Our next flight was a domestic flight from São Paolo to Brasilia. After retrieving my luggage, we boarded a bus heading west to Abadiânia. It had taken more than 22 hours to reach the airport in Brasilia. We were almost there. On the bus I kept looking out the windows at the barren landscape. "What are those strange looking mini-Egyptian pyramids on the ground?" I asked loudly to the group. Josie replied, "The Brazilians call them termite condos. They're made from dirt." My mind began opening to this very foreign country. Two hours later we reached our final destination, Pousada Catarinense.

We each found our assigned rooms. Mine had a single bed, chest of drawers, and a wall that opened into my bathroom. I barely had enough room for my scooter to turn into the bathroom from my living area. The bus driver placed my suitcase near the front door on the floor. I unzipped the bag, grabbed my toiletry kit and drove back into the bathroom to brush my teeth. Rather than unpacking my bag, I decided to live out of my suitcase. I had more important work ahead of me than organizing my clothes. After pushing some furniture around so I could more easily maneuver my scooter, I drove to the dining hall. Several tables surrounded the rectangular buffet cart. This must a foreign country; I did not recognize most of the entrées. I had never seen mangos this large. They were yummy. After eating lunch, I drove my scooter to The Casa.

It was quite peaceful "walking" around and seeing the different rooms of the facility. I spent a few minutes reflecting on why I made this trek - wanting to experience the miracle of walking again. That evening, nineteen people from all walks of life met together in Josie's room. She helped us understand what to expect on the days João saw people at The Casa: Wednesdays, Thursdays and Fridays. We all introduced ourselves and told everyone why we traveled to Brazil. Karen and her son Zack were spending time together after she was diagnosed with ovarian cancer. Allen led Wilderness Programs focusing on sweats and purification ceremonies. He was very quiet yet thoughtful when he introduced himself. Trish and Carolyn were both looking for miracles to help cure their cancers. I finally met my match with Trish. I felt her positive energy. She enjoyed talking about herself and what she expected to accomplish while in Brazil. Her attitude was beyond belief for someone who was told she had Stage 4 ovarian cancer and three months to live. Mike and Jamie were father and daughter looking to strengthen their relationship. He was a very large man with huge hands. No wonder he was a massage therapist. Tom was a successful physician in New York City who was looking to deepen his spirituality after suffering a heart attack. He was very well read on healing methods and meditation techniques. Valerie was a successful business owner who traveled the world as a handbag designer. Her daughter Laurelle joined her for the healing experience. Barbara, Merlyn, Valerie and Wayne were all deepening their understanding of spirituality. Lynne helped individuals and small groups using energy healing and guided imagery. She was intense but knew how to heal other people. Camillia just didn't feel right and wanted some direction from João. This time together was a great introduction for me into opening my mind to other possibilities.

After these introductions, Josie sang and chanted some Native American songs that she had written. We were all strangers looking to accomplish different objectives but had one common bond. We all wanted to experience the healing powers of João de Deus.

In addition to Josie being our translator and tour guide, she also provided us with extracurricular activities. On our second evening in Brazil, she took us on a one-hour taxi ride to meet a man named Mr. Lima in Anapolis. This man was a trance medium painter whose body incorporated certain past master painters. Before entering his trance, he told us he had painted over 51,000 paintings of flowers with no two being the same. Each of us wrote down the number of paintings we wanted to purchase. He turned on his tape recorder that played classical music and entered his trance. It was wild to watch. His whole body shook and then he had a blank look on his face. Over the next two hours he painted more than 60 canvases using his fingers for brushes. I was in total disbelief. "Is this for real?" I asked one of our group members.

Each painting used unique colors that personalized the canvas with subtle healing powers. Different colors had different meanings.

For example, pink and red represented the heart and the circulatory system. Yellow represented solar energy and the balancing of the nervous system. White represented purity. I believe Josie had an alternative motive for our group seeing this man in action. She wanted us to open our minds and experience the energy of incorporation and healing before our sessions with João. What a great tune up!

8

DO YOU BELIEVE IN MIRACLES?

The next morning I prepared for my first day at The Casa. My cousin told me that everyone wore white clothes during the three days of sessions with João each week. This surprised me but I wanted to fit in with everyone else. "Why should it matter what you wear?" I thought to myself. She told me the main reason for wearing white was being sacred and pure in the presence of the Entity. On the road from our pousada towards The Casa, it was a sea of white clothed people. Never in my life had I seen anything like this. It was exciting and exhilarating to see so many people all focused towards the common goal of spiritual healing. While most people walked, there were many buses outside of The Casa. Many people spent all night on these charter buses traveling from rural Brazil to experience the healing of John of God.

Josie told us during our orientation there would be four lines of people congregating in the main meeting hall. After some general announcements and prayers spoken in Portuguese, João entered the hall on the stage with a man sitting in a wheelchair who appeared to be in a trance. Everyone became very quiet while watching João remove a tumor from this man's scalp without any anesthesia. I heard something drop into a surgical tray. My eyes stared in disbelief. What just happened? After this incredible event Josie told our group this physical operation was very rare but was João's way of demonstrating to people he had miraculous healing abilities. It certainly got my attention.

After this spectacular display, we lined up in our respective lines. The First Time Line filled with people who had never been to The Casa. The Second Time Line included people who received an "X" marked on their photos sent in advance of their healing journey to Abadiânia. The third line was the Review Line for those people returning from their invisible operations. All remaining people lined up in the 8:00am/2:00pm Line for meditation in the Current Rooms.

I lined up in the Second Time Line since I previously sent my picture to João. He marked my picture with an "X" meaning he wanted to see me in person and prepare for an invisible operation during the afternoon session. My fellow group members reacted very differently to my pending operation. Some were very envious. "Why do you get to have an invisible operation and I don't?" Others were very curious and wanted to know how I knew to send my picture in advance of our trip. I shut them out of my mind and focused on me. I felt lucky I was going to have an invisible operation but was also scared. "What is going to happen to me? Would I start walking again?" raced through my mind.

We proceeded in the Second Time Line through the first and second current rooms until we reached João sitting in his chair. I felt a unique, pulsating energy from the people meditating in these rooms. Everyone had their eyes closed, palms pointed up and arms resting on their legs. Relaxing music played loudly in each room. Josie accompanied me and translated her conversation with João. I looked into his eyes but only saw a person who appeared to be somewhere else. Someone was inside his mind and body. He waved me on meaning he concurred that I should have an invisible surgery during the afternoon session.

After lunch I returned to The Casa for the 2:00 pm session. I lined up with others who were mentally preparing for their invisible operations. Our line proceeded through the two main current rooms until we reached the Third Current Room. I followed everyone into the room and parked my scooter towards the back of the room. We were asked to close our eyes and place our right hands on our heart. One of the staff members instructed us to concentrate on what you wanted with your individual healing. We were told some people might feel sensations like tingling or fingers gently manipulating certain areas of the body, while others would feel no physical sensations. In their words, both experiences were normal.

Everyone became very quiet. A staff member then made his announcement, "Everyone keep your eyes closed. You are now going to have an invisible operation." I listened for anything out of the ordinary. "Can I hear these entities performing surgery?" Everything sounded normal to me. Someone entered the room. "Is it João?" was the first thought in my mind. "I have to be a believer," was my rebuttal to wondering what was going to happen. Some people started crying. I did not feel anything being manipulated on my body. After a short while in silence, we were told to exit through the door to the outside. The elapsed time in this room was no longer than 10 minutes.

Josie was waiting for me after exiting the Third Current Room. I felt discouraged because I didn't feel any different. What a strange experience. I had great expectations for immediate results. My mind told me to slow down and relish this moment. She immediately told me, "After filling your prescription for herbs, you need to stay in your room for the next 24 hours. Don't plan on any major activity during the first week after your operation. On the 7th night (next Tuesday night) wear white to bed. Say a prayer before sleeping and keep a cup of water by your bedside for when you wake up." Under my breath I thought, "There are too many rules in Brazil but I want this to work so I am going to follow her directions."

I drove my scooter back to my room for the remainder of the day. After taking a nap, I became very restless. I was supposed to stay in my room and have one of my group members bring me dinner. Needing a break away from my room, I joined some of our group at the dinner buffet. Everyone wanted to know how I felt. "I feel energized," was my quick response. I had not digested the entirety of the afternoon events so I avoided other questions and kept to myself.

Immediately following dinner I returned to my room. Once it became dark, I turned on my reading light and opened one of the books I had purchased from Josie. Josie's writings on spirituality seemed appropriate for my period of inactivity. My dreams that night were wild. I saw former President Jimmy Carter placing his business cards on people's windshields. I also saw myself working at the oil and gas investment bank that employed me in Dallas. Someone hired me to sell Exxon producing properties in Utah. Why could I never stop thinking about business?

When I woke up my neck, back, and legs were very sore. I believed this was a good sign that the entities worked on me overnight. After breakfast, I wrote in my journal about the last 24 hours. It felt so peaceful and very quiet. While parked outside my bedroom, I watched a man traveling via horse and buggy pulling his wagon filled with bricks manufactured at the local brick factory. How surreal. My senses seemed so alive and alert. Several stray dogs barked at the horse. The air smelled so clean and fresh.

After sharing my dreams with Josie, she confirmed me going to the wheelchair area of the Second Current Room. Some people think the purpose of going to Abadiânia is only to see John of God. The current rooms are power-places for spiritual practice, raising vibrations and healing. The term "current" (Portuguese *corrente*) refers to the vital force, or spiritual energy that flows through the room and is sustained by mediums and meditators. Once the session started, everyone was supposed to keep their eyes closed, legs uncrossed and hands and arms out of contact with each other, to allow the free flow of energy. Apparently the Entities cannot work on you if your eyes are open. Josie told us during our orientation, "In the current room, say a prayer of what you want. After saying your prayer, send prayers for others. You should be in deep meditation using guided visualization. Open your heart and practice acceptance and forgiveness. Express gratitude and thank the creator for your life."

At 2:00 pm I entered the Second Current Room and found the wheelchair area against the back wall. Luckily there were oscillating fans whose wind hit me in the face because without air conditioning it was very hot. I thought August was supposed to be cooler in Brazil. Not this year. I had never meditated before so I wasn't really sure what to do with my eyes closed. Visualization was another unfamiliar concept to me. As instructed, I prayed a lot. My mind wandered through many different and unconnected subjects. At one point, the strangest feeling overcame me while praying. My body started to vibrate. Beads of sweat formed on my forehead. Should I open my eyes? It felt like I was being sucked into an energy vortex. Vertigo filled my body with strange thoughts of me tipping over in my scooter. Thankfully the afternoon session ended with an announcement from a staff member. I desperately needed some fresh air.

At our group debriefing after dinner, I described this feeling to Josie. She mentioned that many times you become a "giver" of energy for the entities to use in healing others. I also explained to her that I didn't understand the concept of visualization. Josie responded with another question. She asked me, "What color of vibration do you see as your healing color?" I told her my favorite color was purple.

She continued, "Visualize violet light passing through your body. To protect yourself against being the "giver" of energy, visualize a protective shield covering your body. Place all of your focus on pleasurable thoughts. Focus on what you want to accomplish, step-by-step, focusing on one thing at a time. Think about what would give you fulfillment. What do you want to change? Finally, imagine you are holding a fishing rod with a carrot on the end. Throw the carrot into the future and imagine being drawn to it."

During the morning session I implemented Josie's suggestions. Her visualization techniques really worked for me. First I prayed for the things I really wanted: 1) to walk again unassisted, 2) free my body of MS, and 3) to remove my gluten intolerance. These goals tied into the goals Josie asked me to create before leaving for Brazil. Now I understood why she asked me to go through the exercise. I asked the entities, "What should I do that would give me fulfillment?" The answer that came to me in meditation was to mentor MBA students. I also asked the entities, "What do I need to change?" The answer surprised me but made sense: Have a better tolerance for others. I was always very quick to judge others and could not accept indecision. In one afternoon, I gained new purpose in my life.

The afternoon session was long and hot. I needed to focus on something other than feeling like I was melting in the heat. I used my time in the current room to create additional visualization techniques. My number one priority was walking again. "What do I really like to do that accentuates walking?" It came to me like the other answers provided by the entities. One of my favorite activities during spring break in college was playing beach volleyball. In order to play volleyball I visualized myself springing through the sand, into the air and spiking the ball across the net. I also saw myself playing the game in the hot sun. Since my diagnosis, the heat had been the biggest catalyst for creating symptoms with my disease. When I overheat, my legs tighten up, my arms get heavy and I become extremely weak. Playing volleyball in the sun allowed me to indirectly conquer my disease. A person needs to stand and walk or run in order to spike volleyballs. I also created a method of using Josie's carrot and fishing pole technique. Attached to my fishing pole was a golden carrot. I visualized casting the carrot across a sun-dried riverbed. Once it reached the ground, I saw myself walking across the riverbed to retrieve the golden carrot. I knew these techniques helped me because I no longer felt the energy draining out of me. Instead, I could feel the energy from the current room entering my body through my hands. Lightening rods of energy created pulsating bursts through each finger. My arms felt light and unencumbered by MS.

What an amazing three days. I met people from all over the world with incredible attitudes and healing expectations. It was infectious to be around so many people with the common goals of increasing their spirituality and healing abilities. After only a week in this town, I felt very comfortable telling strangers my story. Everyone understood me and encouraged me to keep building upon my positive attitude. I did not feel disabled even though I couldn't walk – yet. My whole body felt lighter. I sat up straighter and hope filled my thoughts with good things to come.

On Saturday afternoon, Josie introduced us to members of the Fulnio Indian Tribe. She had discovered this tribe during a previous trip to Abadiânia and had befriended them. She was helping them with some of their problems such as drought and famine. The tribe members describe themselves as healers. On Josie's website (www.healingjourneys.net) she provides some background on them: "The Fulnio Indians of the Pernambuco area of northeastern Brazil are only modestly known within and outside of Brazil. They now number less than 6,000 and have lived on their current "reserve" of land for more than 500 years. Their name, Fulnio, means "people near the river." The region where they live has been in a state of drought for more than four years. The rivers are dry and the Fulnio have not had access to water during these years. Cattle ranchers are trying to take half their remaining land away, and some of the local Brazilian townspeople have repeatedly burned and looted the Fulnio homes. And, as with many tribes throughout the world, the impingement of the western world upon their lifestyle has created loss of land and the resultant disruption of a culture based on ties to its land. The Fulnio, despite these many and complex pressures and challenges, have held on to their spiritual and healing practices. Every year for three months they go on spiritual retreat, in order to renew their ties to their traditional ways."

The Fulnio gave our group a private showing of their handmade crafts: ceremonial headdresses, necklaces and other paraphernalia. I purchased a necklace for Jacob made from real monkey teeth. For me, I bought a necklace made from armadillo bone and hardened coconut. I also bought a blowgun with darts and a ceremonial protection necklace made with flamingo feathers and an alligator tooth. Hearing the hardships endured by this tribe provided me with a special fulfillment for paying them money. I also felt an immediate connection with their group leader named Jaguar.

Josie told me before we left for Brazil that our group would watch members of their tribe perform one evening. We watched them dance and sing songs while wearing headdresses and ceremonial paint. Now it was my turn to give back to them. Before leaving for Brazil, I asked each of my kids to think of gifts I could bring with me for the Fulnio children. Sydney gathered all of her Barbie dolls she collected during the last seven years. Jacob provided me several decks of his Yuh-Gi-Oh cards. I was so proud of them! We also bought an oversized bag of candy for their tribe to enjoy. After they finished their songs and dances, I approached Jaguar. "Please provide these gifts to the children of your tribe. You have inspired me and my family to give more than we take." Jaguar responded to me after several minutes of silence and reflection. "Your will is very strong. Remain true to your healing. With God's help, you will walk again." I felt like I was watching him speak from afar. Jaguar touched my heart with his hands and blessed me. My heart raced with excitement, fulfillment and complete disregard for everyone watching me. This moment was amazing and completely unexpected. Wow! This was truly an out of body experience.

After we left their compound, Valerie came up to me and told me I had a very generous family filled with love. I had a hard time focusing on her words. My mind brought me back to Jaguar's conversation. This man saw through me and touched my heart. How could he be so insightful after this one encounter? This town was magical.

On Monday, our group walked to the spiritual waterfall called the *Cachoiera* (Sacred waterfall of The Casa). The water was used for healing, strengthening and cleansing. Josie told me to stay behind since the dirt path leading to the waterfall was steep and rocky. I was disappointed. My background reading about this day trip described many healing stories from the waterfall. I wanted to go. I needed to go. I kept searching for an answer to go with everyone. After much inner reflection, I reluctantly accepted that safety was a higher priority than tipping over in my scooter. The men and women from our group took separate turns bathing in the sacred water. To my surprise, the men collected several water bottles from the waterfall and told me to pour them over my head. I was instructed not to shower for 24 hours after cleansing with this water. Though I cringed hearing another rule, feeling better and walking again motivated me to follow instructions.

Before my diagnosis, I made the rules. I was a leader who barked out orders because something needed to be completed quickly and accurately. Investment bankers had little patience for incompetence or mistakes. I always winced during presentations when I found typographical errors. Following other people's orders or rules did not feel comfortable to me. It was all about control and I was a control freak. Everything changed after my diagnosis. While I tried to control my health through proactive decisions, something was different now. I had no control of my disease. Proactive decisions sometimes worked but sometimes did not. Anger, despair, resentment, uneasiness and uncertainty tried to fill the void. My hope and attitude always brushed these thoughts aside.

After lunch, Tom led a discussion about four different books that linked the power of the mind and healing at one of the outdoor tables at Fruitti's. I was fascinated to hear a traditionally trained physician speak so openly about alternative healing methodologies. There was so much I needed to read and learn after returning from Brazil. Suddenly Valerie quickly stood up. Her white plastic chair tipped over backwards. She saw a curly haired woman dressed in a white, loose fitting cotton blouse walking down the street towards The Casa. "David, that's Patti Conklin. I really want you to meet her. I'm going to ask her if she'll join us," she whispered to me in her British accent. Before I was able to encourage her, Valerie was already sprinting towards this stranger. Two minutes later they were both sitting at our table.

Still dressed in her free flowing white cotton blouse and pants, Patti Conklin had beautiful light brown curly hair and a sunburned face. She smiled and acknowledged everyone at our table. I felt very relaxed sitting next to her.

Patti was a total stranger who already knew me. She knew how many lesions lived in my body. She knew how the disease developed in my body. She knew about the traumatic event that occurred when I was six years old. How could she know these facts? She piqued my curiosity. Our conversation was brief but she described living in Atlanta and working with people as a healer using cellular cleansings. Patti would soon propel me towards the next phase of my healing journey, but not before I tested her insight with my MRI scheduled in Denver when I returned from Brazil.

We met as a group on Tuesday afternoon as we prepared for our next three days at The Casa. Josie was very helpful in addressing some very touchy topics. One of my questions was, "How long do you expect it to take before we see results?" She told us, "Healing is a process. Shifting your DNA takes time. Ask the entities to help you accomplish your goals." Josie also spoke indirectly to our group members who were battling cancer. "Healing is not always about feeling or getting better. For some people, you need to prepare for your exit. You need to consider leaving on your eternal journey. Ask the entities for their help in releasing judgment of people. Tell them you have so much love for all of them."

Bedtime approached so I changed into a white t-shirt and pair of white sweat pants. I followed Josie's instructions and placed a glass of plain water by my bed. After closing my eyes, I gave thanks to the entities and asked them to come and remove my invisible stitches. In the morning I drank the water blessed by the entities and gave thanks.

In the morning I started my current room experience in the Second Time Line. Josie accompanied me through the line. We walked in front of João and asked him if the Entity wanted me to do another spiritual operation. He waved me by with no response other than telling Josie I needed to take three crystal baths. That's it? I wanted more interaction with this man. What a letdown. To say I was disappointed would be an understatement. The voice in my head said, "Slow down. Follow the rules. Be patient." I spent the remaining morning and afternoon sessions in the Second Current Room.

During the morning session, something truly amazing happened to me. While meditating and using my visualization techniques, a message came to me. The words were sitting in my mind. The only thing I could compare it to was the voice in your head. The communication had to come from one of the entities. Who else would send it? They said, "Before you can be healed physically, you must be healed spiritually. We believe you have been healed spiritually." Wow! In less than five minutes, my life became so clear. No more self-doubt, no more questioning my aggressive attitude towards living life. I felt so energized from these words. My eyes opened widely from the rush of excitement. This message made my whole trip worthwhile. All of my personal sacrifices and difficulties traveling alone became very small. Never would I have thought to link spiritual and physical healing. Now I understood the concept of divine intervention.

My success with meditating continued on Thursday. The morning session was very powerful. I could feel the energy surrounding the current room. After saying my prayers and using my visualization techniques, I had another out-of-body experience. The music of Roberto Carlos played over and over. One of his songs, Santa Maria, looped in my mind. He sang all of the words in Portuguese. Even though I could not understand the words from the song, I felt the music resonating in my body. All at once, my body lifted off the seat of my scooter. I could feel the healing energies from the entities moving through my legs, torso, arms and fingers. I had to tell my group mates about this experience during the complimentary vegetable soup with tubular pasta (blessed by the Entity) served after the morning activities.

The afternoon session provided me with two additional unforgettable high moments. I took seriously the notion of keeping your eyes closed while sitting in the current rooms. I was not about to break the rules, especially if it meant the entities could not work on me when my eyes were open. Midway through our session another voice entered my mind. The voice told me to open my eyes. Approximately 30 feet in front of me João was sitting in his chair; the same chair and location he always sat. Standing in line was a man with a companion. The man walked with two crutches secured around his wrists. They stood patiently until João motioned for them to approach him. The man made his way in front of João dragging his legs one at a time using his crutches for leverage. This man listened to the healer incorporating João as he spoke very loudly to them and the audience in Portuguese. The next thing I saw, João took the crutches away from this man and instructed him to walk without the crutches. And he did – up and down the room twice with the crutches lying on the floor. The entities wanted me to see this amazing display of their powers. I needed to keep my faith strong so I could one day stand up and walk without the assistance of my scooter.

The second event happened to me at the end of the current room session. I always waited for everyone else to leave since I needed to turn my scooter around and safely exit without hitting anyone in the crowd. While I waited, a woman who I had never seen before came up to me with a glass of water. She told me, "You have an amazing light around you. You look completely different." I thought to myself, "It must be the energies I've absorbed while in the current rooms." All I could say to this woman was, "Thank you. I feel very full of energy and love."

Once outside, I drove my scooter down the winding sidewalks to the covered lookout veranda. What an incredible day. My belief in myself felt stronger than ever. This town and everyone here lifted my spirits. The landscape around the veranda was so pretty. I panned the hillside while the hot summer breeze blew back my hair. I never imagined my mental transformation would happen so quickly with such intensity. My life prior to Brazil focused on the world revolving around me. In less than two weeks, I found emotions, sympathy, compassion towards others, and the meaning of love. Very cool indeed!

The next day was our final day sitting in the current rooms. After listening to the announcements, I settled into my meditative routine. It took awhile, but again I reached a trance state for several minutes. I heard a buzzing sound in my ears. I felt my body levitating. Weightlessness was an amazing feeling. I floated, I walked, and I followed my dreams playing beach volleyball in the hot summer sun. The afternoon session was uncomfortably warm and without incident. João had been called away to help with an automobile accident. I stayed anyway but was distracted and fidgety sitting in the heat for more than three hours. I was full of prayer. It was time to go home.

On Saturday evening, I stopped at the Internet café to send Andrea a final e-mail. I felt so lucky to have her as my wife that I needed to tell her before returning home. I wrote, *"Dear Andrea: I am so blessed to have you as my soul mate. You have been very patient and supportive of me and that means so much to me. A woman in our group has Stage 4 ovarian cancer and her husband has created such negative energy for her. While here, they talked on the telephone and he told her she was wasting her time. Nothing could be further from the truth. This trip has been special. I really miss you and look forward to seeing you tomorrow."*

Before leaving our pousada on our trip back to the United States, my former uptight next-door neighbor from Germany approached me. She looked like a different person from when we first met. On our second day in Brazil she requested moving rooms because she thought our group needed to settle down and go to bed. We were all so excited we stayed up late and made too much noise for her. I was taken aback by her request and my vindictiveness told me to stay away from her. On our final morning she was approachable and outgoing. She came up to me and said, "You look totally different. You are open." We both experienced healing in our own ways. It felt wonderful to see change occur in someone else. I also felt blessed that others saw the same in me.

My final hour before leaving Abadiânia was a time for reflection. I took a crystal bath and enjoyed meditating and reviewing my fabulous two-week experience. A crystal bed has seven quartz crystals suspended above the bed that align with and correspond to the seven chakras of the human body. A session consists of lying on the bed for approximately twenty minutes while listening to soothing music. The crystals radiate color to the respective chakras to cleanse them and balance their energies. After seven crystal baths over the past two weeks, I felt totally charged and energized. What a great activity to complete my tenure in this magical town.

All of the inconveniences from traveling on a bus and three airplanes over 24 elapsed hours seemed inconsequential. My mind wandered during my elevator ride after the train trip from Terminal B at Denver International Airport. All I could think about was my excitement of seeing Andrea, Sydney and Jacob. When the elevator door opened, there they were. Three smiling and familiar faces. I missed them more than I could ever describe. I was beaming! It felt so good to see them. A big group hug followed. I had so much to share with them.

9

WAKE UP IT'S TIME TO HEAL

My attitude was stronger than ever after returning from Brazil. I had purpose and direction for improving my health. It was now time to focus on physically healing my body. I began pushing my physicians for changes to my treatment protocol. The medicines made me feel horrible and my disease continued to progress. I was willing to feel bad if the treatment stabilized the progression of my disease, but so far the disease kept advancing. I was willing to try anything and nothing appeared to work. It was very frustrating. My neurologist, Dr. John Corboy at the University of Colorado, provided me with an excellent analogy on how someone knew whether the "ABC" medicines were working. "ABC" was the acronym for the FDA approved drugs for treating MS. The purpose of theses medicines was to slow the progression of the disease, and decrease the number and severity of attacks, or exacerbations, when they occur. The "A" stood for Avonex (interferon beta 1-a), "B" Betaseron (interferon 1-b), and "C" Copaxone (glatiramer acetate). Two newer drugs also FDA approved were Rebif (interferon beta 1-a) and Novantrone (chemotherapy drug used by MS patients with secondary progressive MS).

Dr. Corboy told me, "The only way we really know if one of these treatments work is to clone your body and compare the cloned body with the body taking the medicines to see which one is stable and which one declines." With my disease continuing to advance, he believed my disease moved into a secondary progressive condition. Most people diagnosed with MS start out with the relapsing remitting form of the disease. This form means sometimes the disease wakes up and causes an attack, while other times the disease goes to sleep. Approximately 67% of all people with MS eventually move towards the secondary progressive form of the disease. There may be relapses but the disease continues to accelerate causing more debilitating effects.

After a 9-month period of three Novantrone infusions (one every 3 months), I was ready to give up on all of these medicines. I felt nauseous after each chemotherapy treatment with no physical proof I was stabilizing or getting better. My only smiles came from hearing Jacob's laughter. "Dad, your pee turns blue when you take this medicine. How cool!"

My biggest fear of winding up like my mom in a nursing home bed inched closer to reality. The progression of my disease accelerated to the point of not being able to walk. My sister-in-law, Linda, suggested I read a book called The Celestine Prophecy by James Redfield. The message from this book was very clear; there are no such things as coincidences. Everything happens for a reason.

In April 2004, Andrea began working for Dr. Isaac Melamed. He was a combination of immunologist, allergist and pediatrician. She saw that he was treating people with compromised immune systems with a blood product called intravenous immunoglobulin (IVIG). She mentioned to me that people with MS also received these treatments. My first reaction was, "I've got to try this, especially if it can help me feel better." I decided to confirm if this treatment was appropriate for people with MS and contacted Dr. Corboy. He suggested I discontinue the Novantrone infusions because my disease continued to progress without any proof of benefits from the infusions. He did, however, want me taking one of the ABC therapies so I began three subcutaneous shots per week of Rebif.

The following month I began IVIG treatments through my neurologist. He administered 18 grams once per month. The treatment was supposed to "jump start" my immune system by infusing antibodies from people with healthy immune systems. After my first treatment I requested a follow-up appointment with Dr. Corboy. Andrea told me Dr. Melamed was using much higher doses of IVIG and I wanted to know why I was receiving such low doses. During my appointment I asked two questions. "First, why are you prescribing 18 grams per dose? Second, what is your expectation for my reaction to these treatments?" His responses were interesting. He said the reason for using the 18-gram dose was there was only one IVIG research study performed on people with MS and 18 grams was the dose used in the study. He then told me his expectation with this treatment was that over a 2-3 year period, I would not get any worse. Hearing the second answer was unacceptable to me. I wanted to walk again and feel better. That was all the motivation I needed to start the process with Dr. Melamed.

Before leaving for Brazil, Dr. Melamed performed a number of blood and allergy tests. On my first full day back in Denver, he scheduled an MRI in the morning and an afternoon follow-up appointment to hear the test results. I was very curious about the MRI. I wanted to know if Patti Conklin's second comment to me about the number of lesions on my brain was accurate.

When I entered the room with the MRI equipment, I asked the technician, "Would you please tell me how many lesions you see on my brain during the test?" I did not want to tell her how many lesions Patti saw since I did not want to bias her answer. I hated these tests. Even with earplugs, the banging of the magnets was extremely loud. It was hot inside the tube and you had to remain motionless. At the conclusion of the test, the technician entered the room to help me back on my scooter. "Do you remember how many lesions you saw?" She replied back, "We think we see eight, but there may be one overlap." I shook my head with a big grin on my face. Unbelievable. Patti told me she saw seven lesions on my brain and two on my spinal cord. She did see people differently. There was no doubt in my mind.

The results of the blood and skin tests were also interesting. The allergy test was a scratch test to determine my food and environmental allergies. From previous tests I knew I was allergic to mold, grasses, trees and weeds. Amazingly, the test showed negative for everything. Dr. Melamed then looked at my blood test results. One of the blood tests showed my T-cells were completely inactive. He had never seen anyone with T-cells measuring so close to zero. In his opinion, my immune system was not working and completely shut down. I also explained to him I never got sick. He agreed this contradicted someone with a shut down immune system.

In September, my treatment protocol became much more aggressive than with my neurologist. I was administered 180 grams of IVIG (10 times the dose) over a three-day period every three weeks. Now I had a plan. It was exciting to fantasize about walking again. All I needed was time to let my immune system wake up.

My first treatment did not start out too well. It took two nurses and six attempts to find my vein for the IV. After this first dose, I was able to lift my right leg better. I also experienced more energy. After being stuck six times with the needle for the IV, I demanded we try something different before my next infusion. The morning before the infusion, I went to the hospital and had a "PICC Line" installed. A peripherally inserted central catheter is a long, thin, flexible tube inserted into one of the large veins of the arm near the bend of the elbow. It is then pushed into the vein until the tip sits in a large vein just above the heart.

Before my third infusion, Dr. Melamed and I reviewed my latest blood work. He told me the blood work showed something amazing. In September, my anti-myelin antibody read positive. This was normal for someone with MS since the disease destroyed myelin. Within the last month, this reading turned negative. "Does this mean we've turned off the disease?" I asked. His response to me was, "Possibly."

The latest blood work also showed an elevated liver function. Dr. Melamed and Dr. Corboy discussed this result and they agreed to take me off the Rebif since that was most likely causing my liver fuction to elevate. I was ecstatic. No more shots three times a week and feeling flu-like symptoms after every shot.

Over the next four months, I tried four different IVIG products (Panglobulin, Carimune, Polygam and Gamunex). Apparently each mixture used different filtering mechanisms to create the product. Every person reacted differently to the various mixtures. We had to find the mixture that provided the benefits I was looking for: increased energy, strength and flexibility. If my insurance company paid for these treatments, I didn't care about changing mixtures. I was very fortunate to have a Group EPO Plan with Empire Blue Cross Blue Shield. My insurance company reimbursed each three-day infusion for approximately $14,000.

After six rounds of these treatments I did not feel any different - no better, no worse. However, the PICC line became problematic. Yes, it was better than being poked up to six times to find a good vein. Especially since my treatments were scheduled every three weeks for three consecutive days. In order to take a shower, I had to wrap the PICC line with Saran Wrap to keep it from getting wet. One weekend morning, I asked Sydney and Jacob to help me wrap my arm before my shower. "Dad, can we wrap you all the way around your body?" All I could do was laugh out loud. "You goofballs, how am I going wash my hair with both arms wrapped to my body?" We all giggled. I cherished these moments of laughter to counterbalance my daily hassles.

Knowing these treatments would continue for the unforeseen future, I wanted a more permanent solution. A MediPort Catheter provided the solution. The device is implanted under the skin with a connecting catheter that is threaded from the port into the jugular vein, through the chest, to just above your heart. It provided an easy way to draw blood and administer the IVIG treatments. Another problem solved. Now I could take showers without concern for the MediPort getting wet since it was installed under my skin. There was also less risk of infection as compared to the PICC line. But the risk of infection still ranked as one of the highest risks. An infected MediPort posed a higher risk of septicemia since it could spread bacteria through my bloodstream into central circulation. Septicemia can be rapid and life threatening. I thought I understood these risks and cast them aside since I did not believe they could happen to me.

After my Mediport day surgery, we traveled to Crested Butte for a weeklong ski trip with Andrea's sister Laura, husband Steve and their two daughters. We rented a large house and were welcomed by a blizzard upon our arrival. Unfortunately Jacob caught a stomach virus on the eve of our final day. After staying up all night listening to him moan and vomit, we decided we had enough fun and drove back to Denver. We were all exhausted on New Years Eve, so we went to bed early. After midnight, it was my turn for the stomach virus. This was the first time I vomited since being diagnosed with MS in 1998. Never in my life was I so happy to be sick. I caught the stomach virus from Jacob. This was the second indication that my immune system was beginning to wake up and work normally.

During the next five months, I completed seven more rounds of IVIG treatments. Dr. Melamed continued to experiment with IVIG products (Flebogam, Octagam and Octagam plus Albumen). I appreciated his positive attitude toward me feeling better – eventually. But after thirteen rounds I began losing my patience. Each treatment took between 5 and 7 hours for three consecutive days. Luckily I was able to bring my computer to the Infusion Center to work on presentations, make follow-up sales calls and check my e-mails. The Infusion Center also installed a wireless Internet server that helped me work more efficiently. My employer was very supportive of these treatments and my time away from the office. I felt guilty that I was abusing this time off – especially since I did not feel any different than I did nine months earlier. There was no documented proof that these treatments would work. My blood work demonstrated that I needed to wake up my immune system. But even Dr. Melamed could not explain why I didn't feel any better. He continued to believe it was only a matter of time.

My time in Brazil elevated my hope towards feeling better. My time in Brazil helped me find true acceptance with my disease and my physical limitations. I often reflected back to Jaguar's words of remaining true to my healing. I knew I would walk again. Only time and patience would prove me right. But the IVIG treatments challenged my commitment. All of these months of hoping for better days without feeling better. My boss believed in me. My family, friends and colleagues believed in me. While my attitude stayed strong on the outside, my inner being challenged my resolve.

On Sunday, June 5th, my cousin Betsy came to our house for dinner. She was in Denver for a consulting project. I described to her my frustrations on lack of response from the IVIG treatments. "What do you think I should do? I'm willing to try anything but some times a person has to be realistic and make an educated decision based on the facts." She replied to me, "Why don't you ask Patti Conklin? Maybe she can read your energy and give you her opinion on what to do next."

The next day, I sent Patti an e-mail describing my situation, asking for her advice on continuing my IVIG treatments. I got no response. I wondered if she even remembered me from Brazil. The following Monday I started my 14th treatment. I brought my computer with me because I wanted to stay caught up on e-mails before leaving for our family vacation to California. On my third day of treatments, I prayed Patti would respond before our road trip. Unfortunately, the wireless server at the Infusion Center was inoperable. They assured me it would be fixed by mid-morning. The server finally started working again around 4:00 pm. "Why not check e-mail one last time before vacation," I said to myself after completing the treatment. Once booted up and online, I shook my head in disbelief. There it was, Patti's response to my questions.

"Dear David, I thank you for writing to me. I'm sorry its been so challenging for you. It sounds as though you've been using a lot of different protocols and it feels like all of the right stuff; you just seem to be 'stuck' however, almost stagnate. Yes, I do think a cellular cleansing would help you. I will actually be in Colorado doing a cellular cleansing with two people on June 28th and 29th. You are welcome to join us. The cost would be $2,500 and it would be in Vail. If you would prefer something on your own, then I will be in the Denver area on June 25th and 26th, and could squeeze you in. That would be by yourself and the cost would be $3,000. This includes 6 months of follow-ups as it takes that time for your body to completely readjust. A woman that I worked with had Muscular Dystrophy, diagnosed at age 6, in a wheelchair by age 35 and did her cellular at age 44. She was walking in just a few hours. Within 10 days, she had given up her wheelchair etc. While not everyone has those results, I have absolute faith in our body's ability to heal, and heal quickly, once we get the emotional blockages out of the way. We could also do a half hour session, but I really think the intensive work would be better. If you have any questions, please feel free to call Janice at 888-376-3301. I look forward to speaking with you. Many Blessings, Patti Conklin. "

I hurried home after reading this message. My adrenaline started rushing. I felt connected with Patti. "You are not going to believe this," I told Andrea once inside our house. "I finally heard from Patti this afternoon." I then excitedly explained her response. What took me aback were the dates she was available in Denver. Patti said she would be in Denver on June 25th and 26th. We're returning from vacation on the 24th. This cannot be a coincidence. Linda's book recommendation proved right again. Someone above watched over me. There was a perfect reason for both of us to be in Denver on these dates. Somehow, Patti knew.

10

CELLULAR CLEANSING

It was time to disconnect from work and leave on our family road trip to Oxnard, CA. No voice mails or e-mails for 10 days. I had ruined enough vacations as an investment banker. Nine years earlier, I had learned my lesson the hard way.

For that trip, the brochure for the Sandals All-Inclusive Resort in Turks and Cacaos looked fabulous. It looked even better in person. One hundred foot palm trees lined the walkways from the cabanas to the white sandy beach. Watching the waves crash in the turquoise water provided a wonderful escape from my daily 12-15 hour grind at work. The day before we left on the trip, a former client called and engaged my firm in their $150 million acquisition of oil and gas properties. They wanted us to raise 100% of the capital since the value of the properties appeared higher than their negotiated price. The year before, we opened a new office for Canada's largest investment bank. Being a new entrant in the competitive Houston market, we did not have the luxury to pick and choose opportunities. If someone wanted to hire us, we put all of our work aside at the chance of earning a nice success fee. We needed to justify our existence with our home office in Toronto. "But what about vacation?" Andrea pleaded. "I'll take the information with me and work while the kids take naps."

After breakfast, I told Andrea I would meet her and the kids at the beach in 30 minutes after my conference call. Three hours later, I looked everywhere on the beach and finally found them at the pool. Andrea had a very disappointed look in her eyes. "You're supposed to be relaxing," she lectured me. I spent our entire "vacation" on the telephone working on the transaction. Unfortunately the deal never closed. The company's due diligence discovered the value of the properties was significantly below their offer price.

I lost credibility with Andrea and wasted a significant amount of time. Checking voice mails and e-mails every day kept me too connected with work. My salary and bonuses offered many advantages to our family. We bought a nice house in a stable Memorial neighborhood. We had more money for collecting art. We also took nicer vacations to far away locations. Yet I constantly battled with myself over the time away from home and broken family commitments. It took moving to Denver to appreciate the importance of disconnecting from work to relax and enjoy quality time with my family.

We packed in the evening since we planned on leaving for California early in the morning. Packing was no fun for Andrea. It was hard enough thinking about the clothes necessary for one person. She packed for our entire family. I provided no help other than telling her what I wanted to wear. I felt useless not gathering my own clothes since my scooter would not fit in our closet. I always packed my own suitcase before losing my ability to walk. Dependency on others was hard for me to embrace being a disabled individual. I purposely chose an electric scooter over a manual wheelchair because I wanted the control of getting around without asking anyone for help. I offered Andrea limited moral support while Patti's recommendation consumed my thoughts.

The week before we left on vacation, I attended an appointment at the University of Colorado's Pain Management Clinic. The pain in my lower back kept me awake at night. I had intense pain regardless of whether I slept on my side or my back. I did not want another operation but I needed to stop consuming Advil like they were M&M's. The stresses from the surgery to install my intrathecal baclofen pump caused me to lose my remaining mobility. The pump alleviated the severe stiffness from spasticity in my arms and legs but the stress accelerated the progression of my disease. Within three months of the surgery, my walking worsened to the point of falling too often on the pavement and concrete. These unsafe events forced me to use my scooter full time.

A regular x-ray on my back did not provide the doctors enough information. They wanted me to come back for a MRI to help them determine where they should inject the cortisone shot. They also prescribed adhesive pads laced with pain medication for pain reduction. I scheduled the test for the week following our vacation.

After a large cup of coffee and a hurried bowl of cereal we left on our first of two days driving. Andrea and the kids slept during our drive through the Rocky Mountains. I wished I could sleep so easily. The sunrise offered brilliant red, orange and purple colored clouds in my rear view mirror. I could not stop thinking of the information I learned on Patti's website (www.patticonklin.com/cellularcleansing.htm). One quote stuck in my head, "Your body has kept a perfect copy of your every word, thought and emotion. They are stored as cellular memories. As a result, you have become what you say, think and feel. Over time, many layers of these memories develop into blockages. They interrupt the flow of subtle energy within your body. This is what produces disease."

It made perfect sense to me. I certainly had my share of suppressed memories from my eye accident. I really wanted to schedule the Cellular Cleansing but the cost gave me reason to pause. Andrea was so supportive of me traveling to Brazil. The money for that trip never interfered with my decision to go. The Cellular Cleansing would cost as much as my trip to Brazil. "How am I going to convince Andrea I need to do this?" I kept asking myself while she slept. The decision consumed me more than fighting the need to pull over and urinate after the large cup of coffee. I tried to rehearse in my mind how I could justify the expenditure. Andrea woke up. We approached Vail after passing Frisco. "Losing My Religion" by R.E.M. played on the radio. She spoke first. "So where are you going to stay while working with Patti Conklin?"

What an incredible woman. Andrea knew I wanted this experience. Why not continue pushing my mind into other realms of possibilities? Brazil opened my subconscious. I felt a connection with Patti from the day we met. Now I wanted to dig deeper and further explore the power of my mind. Once again I needed to take action. After we arrived at the Embassy Suites in Oxnard, I booked a hotel room in Castle Rock, CO for the following weekend.

We had such a good time on this trip. Every morning, Jacob walked through the buffet line and ordered his daily omelet – three eggs and lots of cheese. After two days, the chefs knew what he wanted without him placing his order. Andrea and the kids spent lots of time on the beach while I found a shady poolside table with an umbrella. By the end of the week, I finished "Up Country" by Nelson DeMille. I loved his writing style. He wrote like I thought. We also took day trips to Universal Studios, Hollywood and the Getty Art Museum. We thoroughly enjoyed a real family vacation without cell phones, emails and unnecessary interruptions. Our two-day drive home gave me lots of time to think about my next spiritual journey. Where would it take me?

Patti planned to meet me in my room around 10:00 am. My very inexpensive hotel sat between several fast food restaurants. The noise from the highway traffic sounded very loud. After checking into my room, I drove my scooter around the parking lot to enjoy the beautiful mountains. The sky was so clear and deep blue, I could see the snow capped Pikes Peak to the south. The sun on my face felt really good.

Almost to the minute after I opened my door, Patti walked towards my room. This provided me another example of our connection. I explained my frustration in the lack of response to the IVIG treatments. Patti told me that I must be blocked from further healing. "Once you let go of your past issues, you will regain the flow of energy in your body. You have lots of distant memories that you don't remember. We're going to resolve these issues and put you on the correct path to feeling better."

I turned the seat of my scooter so my feet rested on the floor. Patti asked me to relax and close my eyes. "I want you to imagine a beautiful white marble staircase. Do you see it? Now walk down the staircase and tell me when you reach the bottom." I told her, "I can see the staircase and I'm at the bottom." My mind started racing from the staircase back to Brazil. The voice in my head explained how this visualization work migrated to a higher, more advanced level than Brazil. I knew the visualization methods taught by Josie worked for me in Brazil. My internal confidence grew. I looked over my shoulder and saw the white shiny staircase with a reflection from the sun in my eyes. "What a cool process," I thought to myself.

"Now that you're at the bottom, look for a long narrow hallway. Do you see it? As you look down the hallway, there should be doors along the right side of the hall. Each door represents one year of your life. Do you see the doors? Every time you open a door, the room will be very dirty. The rooms contain no people or memories, just dirt. " Patty helped me picture each door. She asked me the color and shape of the doors. The hallway looked very long and narrow. I saw each door with numbers on them. "I see the doors but I have a question for you. How will I remember the first several years of my life?"

"Good question. The wonderful thing about this process is that you don't deal with old memories. You don't have to remember anything because your body has all the knowledge to access every memory. You keep the memories of your life, but you release the painful emotions such as fear, anger, resentment or jealousy. The first time you felt anger, you stored that vibration in your body, even if you were just an infant. I call this a Core Issue. This issue started the blockage. Each time you felt anger in your life, you stored it in the same place. To turn around any disease, whether it came from an emotional, physical or spiritual condition, the Core Issue must be located and removed through the process of Cellular Cleansing.

Your body gives me the recordings stored in your cells and spiritual essence. Remember, most of us can and do "forget" certain details that have taken place in our life. As you continue to store these emotions, you become more blocked until, eventually, you create an illness or disease, emotionally, spiritually or physically. You must clear out these vibrational blockages in order to reverse the manifestation of disease. Does that make sense?"

Yes it did. Patty described so many new words and concepts. It did not take long for my mind to reach information overload. My Brazilian experiences helped me overcome my internal resistance. Now I understood how my disease manifested from the traumatic event when I was six years old. I physically shook my head from side-to-side in disbelief. I have to stop letting my logical, process oriented, technical background overtake my ability to let things happen naturally.

"Let's get back to work. Visualize the first door to your right. Imagine, as you are about to open each door, you have a helper. Your helper can be an Angel or Guides that help you clean each room." First I pictured what my helpers looked like. I remembered from Brazil my vision of the entities flying around the room healing people. These entities came to me and offered their help. Patti continued, " Open the door to your one-year-old room. All you need to see is the amount of dirt in the room. The dirt can take many different shapes and sizes. As you clean, you literally clean out the blocked energies and stored memories within your body. Let me know when you've finished cleaning this room. "

Although awake with my eyes closed, it felt like a dream. My eyes moved rapidly from side to side very similar to rapid eye movement in a deep sleep. I pictured boxes stacked on top of each other in a storage space. The dust almost choked me as I moved the boxes around. As I touched each box, the dirt disappeared. I wore an industrial vacuum on my shoulders with a large, 3-inch tube attached to suck up the dirt. It took a long time to clean this room. I removed all of the boxes. My helpers and I cleaned the room from floor to ceiling. The room glistened. "I've finished cleaning this room."

Patti replied, "Good. Now open the door and walk back into the hallway. Look down the hallway and find your two-year-old room. Enter the room, see the dirt and clean the room. Let me know when you're finished."

We cleaned each room through my ninth birthday. Patti suggested taking a break. "You can open your eyes. I felt some very interesting vibrations in your first nine years. I knew the energy would be strong in your six-year-old room from your eye accident. Surprisingly, I felt an even stronger energy in your four-year old room. What happened?"

It took me a while to think back to the fourth year in my life. I could not remember anything to cause emotional blockage. How strange. How could she feel something from my past with so much significance, again?

After lunch we resumed our work. From this point forward, Patti told me we would open doors in five-year increments. Prior to beginning, Patti asked me a question. "What did the voice in your head say about this process during lunch?" It took me a minute to gather my thoughts. "The voice told me to be enthusiastically skeptical. It's not if, but when the process starts working." Patti replied, "OK, that's good feedback. Keep those thoughts in the back of your mind. Let's continue."

Our afternoon session covered a lot of ground. It took considerably less time to clean the rooms as I moved towards the present day. Once completed, Patti told me, "I have more questions for you. I felt a lot of energy in the room that included your eighteenth year of age. What happened?" I paused and reflected for a minute. How much should I tell her?

"I left for college at UT Austin. The fraternity "rush" parties provided a nice diversion from the administrative burdens of registering for classes with over 40,000 undergraduate students. The college brochure never described competing for classes with thousands of freshman students." I could not believe I was about to share this story.

"On a humid, cloudless, sunny day during the first week of class, I had a serious lapse in judgment. The sweat poured from my body while sun bathing at my dormitory's pool. The flagpole flying the Texas State Flag caught my attention. Completely sober, I thought to myself, that flag would look really cool hanging in my room. In broad daylight, I walked over to the flagpole, took the flag off its pole, stuffed it under my shirt, and proceeded to briskly walk to my room. Before I got to the ground floor elevator, a security guard grabbed me and took me to the management office. Within several hours the management decided their best course of action. They told me to vacate my room and move out of the dorm within three days."

I continued telling Patti this story. "My senseless actions began to sink in while signing the paperwork for a one-year lease at an efficiency apartment near my frat house. What a stupid thing I did. One day I'm living in a 27 story private dormitory with 930 rambunctious co-ed students across the street from campus. Three days later I lived alone and isolated from typical late night freshman activities. I bought a 10-speed bicycle to alleviate the impact of my three-mile commute. The loneliness forced me to study and focus on engineering school. Attending classes and achieving good grades became my primary focus – not partying. What a concept!

Coincidentally, my parents traveled to Austin the following week to see for themselves how I adjusted to freshman life. I told them I moved out of the dormitory. My dad exploded when he learned the reasons why. "Listen up mister. I have a very short leash on you. If your actions don't quickly improve, I'm pulling you out of college and back to St. Louis." All I could do was nod my head and apologize for my actions. "By the way, I've got some more bad news to share with you. Last week, your mom was diagnosed with Chronic Progressive MS."

It took years before the news of her health fully registered in my mind. I attended college 1,000 miles away and only visited at holidays. Every time I came home my mom's mobility worsened to the point of initially needing a wheelchair and eventually being confined to a bed in a nursing home. I felt numb as I watched her health deteriorate. I prayed this never happened to me. Another traumatic set of events in my life. Patti sensed the negative energy before she ever heard these stories.

After a quick bathroom break, we discussed other energy changes felt by Patti. She asked about the room containing years 35-40. "What happened in those years? The energy felt very strong."

"In 1998 at the age of 37, I finally received my diagnosis of Relapsing Remitting MS. It took seven years of symptoms and incorrect diagnosis' before a neurologist finally told me I had MS. I battled a sore neck in Dallas that my doctor told me came from a bulging disk. My left foot dragged while walking in Houston. The doctor thought I slipped a disk in my lower back until the X-ray showed nothing worthy of surgery. My frustration grew each year I battled with another inconvenience. It took time to see doctors and physical therapists. I treated time as a scarce commodity. Every appointment caused me guilt. The voice in my head told me I needed to be at work building my investment banking career. My priorities needed to change - health before work and money."

"We're done for the day." Patti instructed me to take it easy until we resumed the next morning. "Since there isn't a bathtub in this room, I want you to take the Epsom salt and combine it with water to make a paste. Spread the mixture on your legs and around your chest and heart. The purpose of the Epsom salt is to draw out the toxins in your body. You released a lot of toxins during your Cellular Cleansing."

That evening I discussed with my dad Patti's four year old question. "When you were four, your mom had a miscarriage." I did not remember the event but my dad explained the emotional trauma on my parents. The miscarriage caused deep depression in my mom. These negative energies passed emotional and psychological trauma to my brother and me. Wow. How could Patti feel the change in my energy? This example provided me all the proof I needed about the value of the Cellular Cleansing process.

After our phone call, I drove my scooter to Wendy's for a bowl of chili and large French fries. When I returned to my room, I reflected back to our afternoon session. My brain felt over stimulated with memories. Was this experience real? Brazil was so simple compared to Patti's work. I could hardly contain my excitement prior to calling Andrea. "Hi honey. You would not believe my day today." We talked about the marble staircase, cleaning each room and my repressed memories. I could feel Andrea's skepticism. "Are you glad you're there? Do you feel any different? When are you going to be home? We miss you." I told her there was no doubt in my mind. I knew I needed to be here.

Before I turned on my TV, I drove into my bathroom and turned on the hot water in the sink. I closed the stopper and dumped half the 64-ounce container of Epsom salt. After pulling off my shirt, I spread the paste on and around my heart and all over my legs. What a mess! Thank God for housecleaning.

On Sunday morning we started again at 9:00 am. Patti discussed the next phase of the program. "Yesterday we finished cleaning each of your rooms by age. The cleaning process helped you unblock the energies within your body. Today you will create three healing pools. I call them the Forgiveness Pool, Unconditional Love Pool, and Healing Pool. Close your eyes again and visualize three pools next to each other. Think about the surroundings around each of the pools. What does it look like?"

First I created the environment around the pools. The area looked like a jungle with tall trees and lush green ferns everywhere. On the left side stood a curved stairway made from stone. As I climbed upward, each stair connected perfectly with the one below. When I reached the top of the stairs, I heard a waterfall rushing in the background. I walked approximately 50 feet, peeked over the ledge and saw the water crashing down below. I approached the waterfall and noticed an area behind the rushing water. A bench made from stone sat directly behind the waterfall. The bench formed perfectly around my body and provided a headrest for comfort. My feet dangled off the ledge. I sat down and watched and listened. It felt so relaxing to hear the water as it fell down below me. I held out my hand and touched the power of the water. The strength of the water pushed my hand towards my legs.

Through the strands of water I saw the spray where the water crashed into the rocks below. A small lake formed from the accumulated water. I noticed three pools connected to the lake. Behind the pools you could hear the waves from the ocean as they crashed on the beach. The pools spilled into the ocean. Seagulls flew overhead. Beautiful multi-colored parrots perched on the trees in the jungle. I walked down the stairs and over to the pools.

Patti instructed me to jump into the Forgiveness Pool. "Picture this pool with a beach area on the edge of the water. I want you to think about everyone you wronged or felt wronged you throughout your life. Your job is to see these people standing in the pool with water up to their knees. One by one, I want you dip your hand in the water and touch the forehead of each person. After you touch these people they disappear. This process allows you to forgive yourself and everyone else."

My group of people on the beach looked more like a crowd. I included past teachers, former and current clients, my parents, brothers, Andrea and the kids. All of these people had received terse words or negative thoughts from me. The process allowed me to remove the emptiness caused by my mental actions.

Andrea and I had traveled to St. Louis for Thanksgiving the first year we started dating. Our house reeked of smoke from my mom's cigarettes and my dad's cigars. My mom needed help in the kitchen since she could not get around efficiently in her wheelchair. The turkey, stuffing and condiments all tasted delicious. It felt good to have my bride-to-be meet my parents while we enjoyed our family's favorite pastime, eating. We watched football after two rounds of food. The pies from Tippins filled the remaining void in my stomach. As much as I enjoyed Thanksgiving dinner, I craved the leftovers on Friday.

The next day, I opened the refrigerator for lunch and could not find any remnants from dinner. "Mom, where is the turkey, stuffing and everything else from yesterday?" I asked quizzically. That's when my mom informed me she gave it all to the two women who helped in the kitchen. I felt shocked, disappointed and angry with my mom for giving away our leftovers. In my mind, her actions were unconscionable. I dipped my hand in the water and touched my mom's forehead. She disappeared. I worked my way through the crowd of people. The process helped me let go of bad memories and forgive people for my actions or theirs.

Patti continued. "Now that all of the people you identified in the Forgiveness Pool disappeared, I want you to pull yourself out of the water. Walk across the earthen wall to the Unconditional Love Pool. Jump into the pool. Only you can swim here. Stay in the water for as long as you like to feel refreshed with unconditional love."

This pool looked very long to me - Olympic pool long. After jumping in the water, I dove under, held my breath and started to swim the breaststroke. I used the breaststroke when I competed in a mini-Triathlon during the summer prior to my senior year in college. I wanted to see how long I could swim without a breath. I swam the entire length of the pool. I turned around and started the backstroke. After several minutes, I told Patti I finished swimming in the pool. I walked out of this pool onto the beach area. I looked at the waterfall and all of the surrounding flora. I felt totally alive and refreshed.

"OK. Now I want you to walk across the earthen wall between the Unconditional Love Pool and the Healing Pool. This is the pool where you will spend the majority of your time going forward. You can always visit the other pools too. The purpose of the Healing Pool is to use the water to heal your body and soul. Whenever you have an ache or pain, jump into the pool and pour water over the affected area.

Let me give you an example. We know you have seven lesions on your brain caused by MS. Sit in the water in the shallow portion of the pool. Picture your head with a zipper connected at the base of the forehead that goes all the way around your head. I want you to unzip the zipper and pull your head open on a hinge so you can see the lesions. What color are they?" she asked.

"They look radiant red to me with smoke emitting like burning embers," I replied. "What shape are these lesions?" asked Patti.

I responded, "They look round. Each one about one-inch in diameter."

"Good. Now I want you to visualize pouring water over these lesions. As you continue to pour the water, see their colors turn from red to orange, orange to yellow, and yellow to white. You extinguish their heat and turn them from active to dormant. When they turn white, turn your head sideways and watch the lesions fall onto the ground like pebbles or marbles. The power of this pool is your ability to self-heal any area of your mind or body. Does that make sense?"

I took a deep breath and opened my eyes. "Absolutely. But how do you know this process works?"

Patti replied, "Think positive thoughts and continue working in your Healing Pool. Remember what you told me. It's not if, but when the process starts to work. Good things only happen if you want them to happen. You have to tell your mind what you want. If you think to yourself you feel terrible, chances are you will feel terrible. If you tell your mind you will walk again, your mind hears what you want and makes it happen. The power of suggestion is undeniable. When you get home, take a bath every day for seven days using the Epsom salt. Contact me in 30 days, or sooner, and tell me how you're feeling."

On my 30-minute drive home, I reflected on my last 36 hours with Patti. I had a new plan. I felt so excited to begin work in my Healing Pool. Once home, I beamed with joy in front of Andrea and the kids. Over dinner I explained each experience in great detail. I could hardly wait for bedtime to begin the healing process on the pain in my lower back.

That night, I dove into the water and surfaced midway in my Healing Pool. The sounds from the waterfall distracted me for several minutes. In the middle of the pool, I found a seat similar to the one behind the waterfall. I swam over to the seat and sat down in a very comfortable, upright position. The seat fit perfectly around my body. I felt the pain in my lower back and remembered Patti's questions. What shape is the pain? What color is the pain?

I unzipped the zipper along my spinal column. In plain view I saw all of my vertebrae. I focused on the five vertebrae in the lumbar spine called L1 through L5. All five of the vertebrae looked bright red. I envisioned this area in the shape of a 2-inch thick cylinder. It felt like another out-of-body experience as I poured water over the area. I lengthened and extended my arms as I poured the water behind my back using a plastic 5-cup container with a lip.

I felt so confident about this process that I called the University of Colorado's Pain Management Department Monday morning and canceled my MRI. Why bother pinpointing the pain for a cortisone shot when I knew the pain would go away? It took several nights before the pain in my spine changed from bright red to orange. I filled up the cylinder each night until it overflowed. By the end of the first week, the pain vanished. The color in the cylinder looked clear. I wanted the pain to disappear and it did. My work in the Healing Pool proved to me the process worked. If I can make the pain in my back go away, what else can I do?

11

UNFORTUNATE ACCIDENTS

My work in the Healing Pool continued every night. I wanted to walk again and needed to prepare my body and mind through the visualization work in my Healing Pool. I strengthened my legs by pouring the healing water on my leg muscles and saw them as continuous one-inch thick electrical wires. Patti also encouraged me to continue my pool work and Pilates class.

Since the beginning of the year, I'd been participating in a Pilates class designed for people with MS at HealthSouth. The class provided an excellent form of exercise in a controlled environment that included a least one physical therapist. We focused on posture, balance, and core strength. The first thirty minutes of each class we started on a large, elevated exercise mat where we stretched and worked our core strength and abdominal muscles. Exercises included bridges and sit-ups where we used colored Thera-Bands to pull ourselves up into a crunch position. The second half of the class, we used the reformer machines and trapeze tables for additional exercises that focused on core strength.

At our weekly Wednesday class, I explained my Cellular Cleansing experience to my exercise partner (Rick) and physical therapist (Jamie). I could not contain my enthusiasm on the results to date. They had often heard about the pain in my lower back and usually shook their heads in disbelief. Jamie interrupted me, "Dave, I want you to do the plank exercise." In the plank, you start on your stomach with your legs straight. I used my forearms for leverage and pushed up onto my toes, forearms and elbows as the only contact points on the mat. Rick held this position for 6 minutes, 45 seconds without a break. After only two minutes, I fell back on my knees. I told myself I needed to improve my performance with the plank exercise at least thirty seconds every week.

On our way to the reformer machine Jamie asked me, "Dave, what happened to your elbow?" I looked at my left elbow where I saw a golf ball-sized growth on my elbow. It felt squishy but not painful. "I don't know. If the size doesn't recede, I need to see a doctor." After one week without any change in the size of my elbow, I visited my doctor. He told me I burst my bursa sac and created a condition called bursitis. "The fluid will dissipate over time. Cosmetically, you can reduce the size of your elbow using a syringe to pull fluid away from the area. The procedure does, however, increase the risk of infection at the point of the inserted needle. Unfortunately, I cannot guarantee the fluid won't return."

After one week, I returned to my doctor to drain my elbow. Sydney and Jacob felt extremely disappointed. They enjoyed playing with the squishy ball at the end of my elbow. Unfortunately, ten days passed and the fluid returned as my doctor suggested could happen. Once again, my doctor drained the elbow. Luckily I had no pain at or around the bursitis. This time, however, he could not pull any fluid through the syringe. He told me, "I'm sorry I couldn't make your elbow look any better. Hopefully this means the fluid and inflammation should dissipate quickly on its own."

In between these two doctor appointments, Andrea flushed my mediport with saline and heparin since I discontinued the IVIG treatments the previous month. The port had to be flushed once per month to keep the line open and reduce the risk of infection. At this point, I did not want to remove the port. I wanted to keep my options open in case I resumed the infusions at a later date. My immunologist provided us all of the necessary materials to flush the port at home since Andrea was a Registered Nurse.

At the end of the week, I left work early to attend a prospect's 50th Corporate Anniversary Party for employees, clients and guests. They could not ask for better weather for the outdoor party. The sky showed a deep, dark blue without any clouds. I still felt hot even though I stayed in the shade. Luckily the sun moved behind their building. After several speeches, the crowd formed lines for Bennett's Barbeque. I originally passed on the food since I did not want to spoil my appetite on days Andrea cooked dinner. The food smelled wonderful. Their grills poured out the smells of long-term smoked meats. My willpower wavered. I had to sample the brisket, hot links and smoked turkey. After a quick plate of protein, I left the party to start my cross-town 60-minute Friday afternoon commute.

As I entered my car, it felt like I walked into an oven. I had parked in front of the wrong building and the parking lot fell directly in the afternoon sun. Sweat poured from my head. I'm glad I had hand controls in my van because my legs felt weak. Sixty minutes with the air conditioner cranked should cool me down.

By the time I reached my neighborhood, my body felt better. No more sweat or weakness in my legs. I took a right hand turn into our subdivision. On the cul-de-sac to my right, several kids played in the street. With so many kids outside, I knew I needed to be careful and slow down as I reached my cul-de-sac on the left. I looked to the right down the main street for cars and kids. Nothing. I looked to the left and saw my next-door neighbor's son Jackson and his friend standing on top of the sewer grate. Why were they standing so close to the busy main street through our neighborhood?

Seeing these kids so close to the intersection put me on full alert. I looked to the left as my car inched towards my house. The last thing I wanted was one of these boys running in front of my car. It never occurred to me to look to the right as I drove forward. As my eyes darted from the front of my car to the sewer on the left, my eyes blinked for a split second. As I looked back towards the front of my car, a very strange feeling overcame me. Why was Jackson's four-year old brother Jason riding his bike in front of my car? Could this be a dream? By the time I realized the reality of the situation, I heard a thud along with tremendous screaming. I had hit Jason on his bike.

I shook my head quickly from side to side to wake up from this nightmare. Jason's mom sprinted towards the screams. As Carmen tried to pull Jason out from under my car, his screams shook my world. How could this happen? I rolled down my window. I felt helpless since I could not open my car door, run to the front of my car and help Jason. Hand controls increased my mobility and allowed me to continue driving. Yet my legs didn't work and that became obvious while I yearned to pull him out. At that moment, I felt very handicapped. Carmen calmly said to me, "Dave, you need to back up. Jason's bike and legs are pinned under your left front tire." I put my car in reverse and inched backwards. Immediately I heard a crunching noise. Was that Jason's leg? What was that sound? After Carmen pulled out Jason and clutched him tightly in her arms, next came the mangled bike. The front tire bent at a ninety-degree angle. Sirens blared in the background. Someone had called 911.

Within minutes, the Highlands Ranch Paramedics arrived. Soon after, a police car pulled into my driveway. I thought to myself, "Will I be arrested?" Thankfully, Jason appeared OK. The paramedics told me the boy had lots of road scrapes on his legs but everything looked all right. They recommended Carmen take him to the emergency room for x-rays of his legs. For the next 30 minutes, the sheriff interrogated me on what happened. He also spoke with several people who witnessed the event. At the end of this surreal interview, the sheriff told me he would not issue me a ticket for my actions. My story checked out with the witnesses.

It took several hours before I settled down. My heart raced. I needed a stiff drink. I could not believe I hit Jason on his bike. At 9:45 pm, our doorbell rang. Jason and his dad John stood at our front door. Andrea invited them into our family room where I sat on my leather chair. "We just returned from the emergency room." John told us. "No broken bones." What a relief. Jason still had on his cowboy boots and shorts. The first words out of his mouth made me want to cry. "Aren't you going to tell me you're sorry?"

"Jason, I am so sorry. I've been worried about you for hours. Show me your cuts. Can you move your legs OK?"

"Yeah. I'm OK. The x-ray machine was really cool. They gave me three lollipops and some cool stickers."

The next day we bought Jason a new bike. It took several days before I could describe this nightmare to anyone. I could not sleep. Finally, I sent Patti an email and described the accident. I needed help from this traumatic event. Later in the week she replied to my message.

"Dear David, I can only imagine. It is a parent's worse nightmare. But as in all things, we as souls, even if it is a four year old, have contracts and commitments to each other. The little one is fine. Take yourself to the forgiveness pool and forgive yourself. Also make sure you put the four year old in there with his parents. We are all intricately involved. I will work with you tonight while you sleep. Please do the Epsom salt bath if possible and remember to get in the Healing Pool. Only take yourself in there, not the little one. Everything has a reason. Sometimes we just don't know for a while why something happened the way it did. You were being cautious.

You did what you could. Now forgive yourself and the little guy. As I said, I'll work with you tonight, to readjust you. Write to me on Sunday or Monday and let me know how you are doing. Okay? Much love to you. Patti."

Three weeks passed and I still felt haunted by the accident. Over and over, I kept rewinding my mental tape of the event trying to figure out what to do differently. I could not let go. I could not sleep more than one or two hours without waking up. Once awake, it took several hours before I fell back asleep. I continued to relive the accident over and over. At Patti's suggestion, I used my time awake and jumped into my Forgiveness and Healing Pools. I included Jason's parents in the Forgiveness Pool to confront my anger. I could not let go of my anger at them for allowing Jason to play unsupervised at the intersection of the main neighborhood street and our cul-de-sac.

The accident also affected my daytime routines. One day after driving home from work, I pulled my van into our garage. I proceeded to drive my scooter from inside my van onto the lift that lowered me to the garage floor. I parked my scooter next to the four steps that led into the laundry room of our house. The steps had handrails on both sides. After I climbed the steps and entered the laundry room, I used the washer and dryer on the right and our sink on the left as leverage as I worked my way towards my walker parked in the hallway. Only this day proved different. My legs would not pick up after each step. I had to use one hand to lift my pant leg onto the next step. After I reached the top of the four steps, I lost my balance and fell backwards. Luckily I grabbed the rails as I fell and slid step-by-step down until I stopped under the front tires of my car. Fifteen minutes passed before Andrea wondered why I was not already in our house. She saw me on the garage floor and immediately sounded worried. "Are you alright? Did you hit your head?" Luckily my negative responses alleviated her concerns. I told her with a smile on my face, "No major structural damage! My back scraped on the stairs on my way down. Otherwise I think I'm OK. I could use your help rearranging my legs so I can pull myself upright and back onto the stairs."

Two days later I experienced another dramatic fall in our laundry room. This time my fall occurred while I tried to exit the laundry room onto the four steps in the garage. I always left one of my canes leaned up against the door jam in the laundry room. I used the cane to help me negotiate the twelve-foot walk from the hallway to the door of our garage. My feet felt so heavy. It felt like I had cement blocks attached to each foot. Once again I lost my balance after my legs would not lift up. The cane flew out of my hand as I crashed into our washer and dryer. Andrea heard the thud. "That's it. We have to find a new way in and out of the house for you. I am not going to let you fall anymore as you try to enter or exit the laundry room"

Andrea and I discussed why I fell more often than normal. "What do you think is going on?" I told her I did not feel right. My energy level had decreased. The spasticity in my legs increased. I questioned whether I jarred the catheter of my intrathecal baclofen pump loose from one of my recent falls. Maybe the dose needed to be higher. I wondered out loud if I could be in the middle of an exacerbation. I certainly experienced enough stress over the last four weeks. We decided I needed to visit my neurologist and determine if a round of steroids might alleviate these symptoms.

I visited Rae, the Nurse Practitioner in the Neurology Department of the University of Colorado on Monday afternoon. "Let's make the assumption you're having an exacerbation. It's not necessary to confirm the diagnosis with a MRI. I want you to start a round of five days of steroids. You can receive the first round here at the hospital. I'll set up the treatments so you can do the remainder of the infusions at home. You should start to feel better tomorrow." During her examination she tried to bend my arms and legs. "You feel really stiff. Do you want me to increase the dose on your pump?"

I answered, "Please. I can't bend my legs at all."

Rae said, "OK, I'm going to be aggressive and increase your daytime dose by 20%."

Unfortunately, the steroids did not help me feel any better. I finished the last of the infusions on Friday after work. Why did I still feel so bad? This really sucked. I had done everything humanly possible to confront my disease head-on. When my right foot would not lift up and down on the accelerator on my car, I installed hand controls. When I fell too often at work and home, I fought through the mental roadblocks of how people might view me differently as I drove a scooter instead of walking like a "normal" person. I knew the right thing to do so I went through the insurance approval process and procured a three-wheeled scooter. One day after I drove to work, I attempted to transfer from my Honda Pilot's front seat to the rear of the car to lift my scooter out of the back compartment. I used my walker for the short trip to the rear of the car, fell backwards and hit my head on the concrete floor of the garage. This fall caused a concussion that gave me headaches for a week. Soon after I bought a full sized Ford E-250 Van with a Braun Vangator II lift system to safely get in and out of the van. While I always fought with myself over whether I rolled over and gave into my disease, common sense always prevailed. I used every accommodation available to make life easier and safer. Unfortunately, my frustration climaxed at home on Saturday afternoon while I sat on my leather chair and watched TV with Sydney.

12

CRASH AND BURN

The Labor Day weekend arrived at a perfect time. I needed the three-day weekend to feel better. The last week proved extremely hard on my body both physically and mentally. I thought the steroids would help ease my physical challenges. Unfortunately I still felt terrible on Saturday. My attitude wavered as the weekend began. Sometimes I was tired of trying so hard. Even with all of the accommodations to make life easier, my body still revolted. While frustrated and impatient to feel better, I pictured my mom in her nursing home bed. I never heard her complain. I needed to wake up and stop feeling sorry for myself. Thoughts of my mom gave me strength through these MS moments.

Saturday afternoon Sydney and I watched "The Bad New Bears" with Walter Matthau and Tatum O'Neal on HBO. I sat down on my leather recliner. Sydney helped me lift my legs onto the ottoman. A perfect, thoughtless movie proved just what I needed for an afternoon activity. At the end of the movie I tried to stand up and transfer to my scooter. I really needed to go to the bathroom. I could not move at all. My body felt locked up. After several unsuccessful attempts, Andrea suggested I call my neurologist and ask for advice. The neurology resident at the University of Colorado called me back. "I can't move. On Friday I finished five days of IV steroids and I still feel horrible. What should I do?" After the resident heard my fact pattern, she told me, "Check into the University Hospital Emergency Room on 9th and Colorado. When you arrive at the hospital, the ER will page me."

The hospital was the last place I wanted to go on Labor Day weekend. First I had to get there. At the moment I could not move and really had to pee. Andrea called our next door neighbor for help.

The two of them stood on each side of my chair and lifted me onto the scooter seat. My paralysis distracted me away from the urgency to go to the bathroom. I managed to drive my scooter out our front door and down the three aluminum ramps.

We loaded into my van. Sydney and Jacob sat on the rear bench seat. "I know it's unsafe, but I have to stay in the scooter seat. I really cannot move my arms and legs. That said, please hurry because I desperately need to use the bathroom." It took every ounce of strength to hold my body upright as we drove towards the hospital. I lost my balance several times and almost tipped over on left and right turns of the van.

After we arrived at the ER, a male nurse admitted me into the hospital. Twenty minutes passed before they took me to a treatment room. I begged the nurse to help me urinate. It took two attempts with the Foley catheter but finally I felt relief from my bladder. They also drew several tubes of blood. The nurse told me, "I'm sorry but we won't know the results of the blood work until tomorrow. You need to stay with us overnight. It's going to take awhile to find you a room. Please be patient." I had no problem with an overnight stay. I would do anything to feel better.

Sunday morning an entourage of medical students came into my room with the attending neurologist and the staff neurologist. The group totaled eight physicians. They asked me a bunch of questions to understand my medical history. After the questions, the senior physician spoke to me. "We have some good news and bad news. The good news relates to the blood work from yesterday. We've determined you have a blood infection called Gram Negative Rods. It will take a few more days to determine the specific type of infection. We're going to give you two different IV antibiotics to cover the full spectrum of potential infections. Now here's the bad news. We have not yet isolated the location or cause of the infection. It may take us a few days because of the holiday but rest assured the two antibiotics will kill the infection."

The engineer in me spoke next. "It sounds like we need to eliminate some variables. I don't know how else you can find the cause of the blood infection. I mentioned I had a mediport surgically installed in January for my IVIG treatments. Since I discontinued these treatments in June, why not take it out?" The students all wrote down my request. The group walked out the door. The attending neurologist told me, "We'll get back to you. It may not be until tomorrow"

At least they knew why I felt so poorly. My Type-A, do-it-now personality woke up. I wanted them to be more proactive. I could not accept the 24-hour wait for them to provide their opinion on the mediport. The voice in the back of my head told me there must be some chain of command to make that decision. They had not heard the last from me about removing the port.

Every time a doctor, nurse or student doctor came into my room, they asked me again and again for my medical history. What a hassle. How many times do I have to repeat myself? I felt like their human textbook. Yet their questions gave me another audience to suggest they remove my mediport. I knew it had to be the cause of the infection. Somehow I needed to convince them.

On Monday morning the entourage of students and doctors came back to my room. "We visited with your neurologist, Dr. Corboy. He agreed it makes sense to remove the mediport. We're not sure when it will be removed because of the holiday, but hopefully one of our surgeons can pull it today."

Yea. They finally listened to me. It struck me as odd, though, that I had to make the suggestion several times before they agreed to do the work. Why didn't they come up with the idea? Andrea and the kids visited me later in the morning. She brought me an outstanding lunch. Every year our cul-de-sac neighbors got together for a lobster fest over Labor Day weekend. Each family brought a side dish. While it felt weird not being there this year, the delicious lobster lunch helped lessen the remorse from my absence.

I felt bad that Andrea had to schlep from Highlands Ranch to the hospital every day. While I wanted to spend time with her and the kids, I suggested they only visit once per day. Hopefully they would release me after they removed the mediport. They went home mid-afternoon. Two surgical residents entered my room. "We're here to remove your port." I replied back, "OK. That's great. Do we need to go to an operating room?" Several times after my question the senior resident excused himself to answer a page. His beeper would not stop beeping. He finally returned to my room. "Sorry for so many ins and outs. It's been crazy today. We can take it out in your room unless you don't feel comfortable doing it here." I didn't care. I felt elated they were finally going to remove the port. As long as they created a sterile field I did not care where they performed their work.

After the surgeons created their sterile field, they made an incision at the location of the port. Once they dug around to free the port from skin and adhesions, they pulled the catheter. Luckily they injected me with local anesthetic since it felt very uncomfortable while they dug out the device. The catheter looped from the port, located in my chest approximately 3-4 inches from my right shoulder, through my jugular vein to just above my heart. Within five minutes they finished. A three-dimensional one-inch deep hole in my chest remained as the only remnant from the port. The surgeon told me the hole would take 4-5 weeks to heal because of its depth.

Within 30 minutes of the surgery, my good friend Kirk walked in my room. "Qué paso amigo?" Kirk and I knew each other from Midland, Texas when I worked for Amoco Production Co. as a drilling engineer. Coincidentally, Kirk's wife and Andrea were roommates in Dallas prior to our marriages. Our energetic conversations always covered a lot of ground but led nowhere. Shortly after he asked me a question, I started to hyperventilate. I concentrated on my breathing. Even though my breaths were fast and short through my mouth, I tried to breath deeply through my nose. "Why is this happening?" I thought to myself.

I closed my eyes and walked though someone's house at a party. A lot of people stood around with beers in their hands. Where's Andrea? I couldn't find her anywhere. Why would I be at a party without Andrea? My body started to vibrate as my mind told me I held a four inch thick piece of exposed electrical wire with live current running through it. My palms faced up with my fingers curled around the wire. I saw myself shake violently while being electrocuted. I pleaded to Kirk, "Can't you unplug it? Please make it stop." I heard Kirk tell me, "Dave, there isn't anything to unplug. You're hallucinating."

Later Kirk told me he sprinted to the nurse's station and told them something appeared wrong. A number of nurses ran into my room and took my vital signs. My temperature spiked at 104 degrees Fahrenheit. My heart rate raced to 173. My blood pressure crashed. By the time the nurses cooled me down, I could not move my hands or feet. The sepsis caused me to be paralyzed. My hands faced inward in a position similar to holding something long and circular like a big piece of electrical wire. Kirk called Andrea at home. He told her with a very concerned voice, "You better hurry back to the hospital –

Dave's in trouble." Unfortunately I found the host location of my blood infection the hard way. It resided around my port. When the surgeons removed the port and catheter, the infection dispersed throughout my blood system and sent me into septic shock. Thank God Kirk was in my room when this happened. He saved my life.

The next 24 hours were rough on my attitude. Immediately following my septic episode, the doctors moved me to the step-down Intensive Care Unit (ICU). I needed care around the clock with staff trained for high maintenance patients like me. The next morning, a nurse came into my room and fed me breakfast because I could not even lift a fork or spoon. My eyes swelled with tears. I felt sorry for myself. I prayed my immobile condition would not be permanent. My mind raced to a disabled condition similar to my mom. No. I could not and would not let that happen. Many times I've told people the alternative was unacceptable – my current, temporary, condition.

Later in the afternoon my body started to wake up. I wiggled one of my big toes. I also lifted my left arm a few inches off the bed. By the end of the second day in ICU, one of the nurses told me they planned to transfer me to the Rehabilitation Floor. More importantly, my attitude woke up. I demanded that I stop feeling sorry for myself. I wanted to leave the hospital a stronger person.

But I still wondered why my legs would not work. What changed? Why could I not support my body weight? After several doctors questioned me on my medical history prior to my stay at the hospital, I came up with the answer. My pump. Prior to my most recent exacerbation, Rae increased the dose of my intrathecal baclofen pump by 20% to help reduce my stiffness. But I always responded with significant sensitivity to the amount of this medication. If they increased the dose too much, my legs would not support my body weight and I became very wobbly. My legs would feel spaghetti-like. That had to be the answer.

They moved me to the Rehabilitation Floor on Wednesday. This would be my new home for at least two weeks. They should have renamed the floor the Rehab Boot Camp. There wasn't time to feel sorry for anything or anybody. Every day they scheduled me for one hour of physical therapy, one hour of occupational therapy and one hour of group exercise. All business. They wanted me to push myself and get stronger to the point of going home.

After I returned to my room following two initial evaluations in physical therapy, my telephone rang. "Hi, this is Patti Conklin. Sorry it took me so long to find you. Your cousin Betsy told me about your nightmare. Let's talk about it." Within minutes Patti cut through my emotional energy and told me her opinions. She thought hitting Jason on his bike was the trigger to my septic episode. "How did you feel after the bike accident?" I told her I felt very mad at his parents because he played too close to the intersection. My sleeping became very irregular to the point of needing sleeping pills. I also explained about the hole in my chest where they removed my port. "My nurse told me to expect 3-4 more weeks for the wound to heal because of its depth."

"OK, close your eyes. First, I can feel the anger in your voice. I want you to spend some time in your Forgiveness Pool. You need to forgive yourself, the parents and the little guy. What shape do you see where they pulled the port?" I told her it looked like a cylinder. "What color is your cylinder?" It looked red to me. "That's interesting. I see the same color. Here's what I want you to do. Spend a lot of time in your Healing Pool. Visualize the area where they removed the port as a red cylinder. On top of the cylinder, picture the word ANGER in black letters. Pour water from the pool into the cylinder. See the color of the cylinder change from red to orange, orange to yellow, and yellow to white. Also see the word ANGER disappear as you continue to pour the water. My thoughts are with you. Have confidence in yourself that you will feel better."

Patti's words of encouragement provided me with extra motivation. I went to my Healing Pool at least twice each day while in the hospital. Every waking moment I knew I would get stronger. I wanted to go home but recognized the Rehab Floor was the best place to concentrate on re-teaching my body independence. The attending physician on my floor came into my room one morning. "You are a model patient. You get out of bed early every day and provide us motivation to help you get stronger." My attitude soared.

Every morning one of the nurses came to my room and changed the dressing at the previous location of the port. They took a 2" x 2" gauze bandage and stuffed it into the hole. I hated this experience because they had to pull out the previous bandage that inevitably got stuck on the dried blood in the wound. The pain caused me to cry out as I asked the nurse to stop. They eventually learned to pre-medicate me with Tylenol thirty minutes prior to these painful events.

One morning during the second week of rehab, the nurse questioned what I did to the wound. "What do you mean? Is it getting worse?" I felt energized by his response. "I am shocked. I told you it would take 3-4 weeks for this hole to close over as it healed from the inside out. I cannot even place a 1' x 1" piece of gauze in the hole because it already healed." I grinned. His comments re-confirmed that the Healing Pool really worked. My anger towards Jason's parents also disappeared. I healed my wound through my visualization efforts. No doubts in my mind.

When I first transferred to the Rehab Floor I could not lift my legs at all. On my second day of rehabilitation, my neurologist agreed to reduce the dose of my pump to the level prior to my exacerbation and hospital stay. Within hours, my body responded. During my physical therapy session later that day, the therapist wanted to see my response to their LiteGait System. She hypothesized that by taking weight off my legs I could walk. It sounded good to me. I wanted to walk. A person cannot fall with this body weight support system since a harness connects your body to the upper tubular yoke. After fully connected, I walked approximately 20 feet. Not far, but a step in the right direction.

With practice and three hours of rehab every day, I surprised everyone including me. I felt stronger. On the day prior to my release from the hospital, one of the Physical Therapists wanted to see my progress with the LiteGait machine. She placed the harness on me and asked me to walk. She did not take any weight off my legs through the harness and yoke. I walked up and down the hallway three times. What a boost to my confidence. Now I wanted to go home and sleep in my own bed.

All my efforts and hard work paid off. While not back to full strength prior to my nightmare, I felt strong and energized. I must have told people at least a hundred times about my septic episode. Friends and family always shook their heads in disbelief.

On my last night at the hospital, a surprise visitor walked in my door. Warren was a fellow ACG board member and ran a regional investment bank in Denver. We talked about my septic episode, extended hospital stay, and my progress every day. I tried to limit the number of times I relived the nightmare because my heart rate always increased dramatically. "David, you are so lucky to be alive. You look great with good color in your face. I can hear the strength in your voice. How can you smile after what you went through?" I responded with my typical answer. "Warren, I say this to everyone that asks. The alternative is unacceptable to me. My attitude drives my ability to heal."

13

THE SKY IS FALLING – PART I

It felt so good to be home. My attitude soared. While it took a few days to regain my bearings and feel comfortable sleeping in my own bed, I had no doubt I would continue the progress made at the hospital. Shortly after we walked through our front door, the phone rang. A woman from Centura Home Care called and wanted to schedule appointments with their physical and occupational therapists. No rest for the weary!

Andrea's cooking tasted light years better than the hospital food. She proved it on my first night home. She instructed me sit in my leather chair, close my eyes and relax until dinner. I heard several cans opening, meat sizzling, and the wonderful smell of garlic filling the air around me. My beautiful bride must be cooking my favorite meal – spaghetti and meatballs, Italian sausage, braciole and homemade sauce. Andrea learned to replicate her Italian mom's recipe. She walked up to my chair. "Do you want a taster?"

"Of course I do." Yummy. Fresh out of the oven, I salivated tasting the fresh Parmesan cheese, lots of garlic all mixed together with the ground beef. Andrea shaped the meatballs into bite-size spheres before broiling them in the oven. She knew how to touch my heart, straight through my stomach!

One of the big benefits of working for Marsh was their short-term disability program. The plan paid 100% of my monthly pre-disability base salary for the first three months of an approved disability. It felt comforting to know my income would not be disrupted while I fought my fight to regain my physical and mental strength. While I wanted to get stronger working with the therapists, my goal was to get back to work as soon as possible. I believed that human interaction helped the healing process. I set October 17th as my personal goal for returning to work. Three weeks at home seemed long enough to me.

Each therapist scheduled 2-3 visits per week. By the end of every week, I continued to get stronger. A salesman from Home Depot helped me build a 4-inch high square step out of 2x4's and plywood to practice climbing up and down steps. I also walked with my walker one to two laps from my bathroom, through the hallway, around my family room, dining room, entry way and back to the bathroom. The OT had me molding clay with each hand, picking up different sizes of dry pasta, and working on my core strength through sit-ups and stomach crunches. Rehabilitation felt like a full time job. They drained my energy after each session but I knew I felt stronger every day. I kept a notebook of all the exercises each therapist assigned me as "homework" on the days without appointments. By the end of the third week, the notebook measured one-inch thick. With all these exercises, there wasn't much free time to relax. My internal motivation only understood black or white, green or red, yes or no. I had to slow down. I had to go back to work.

As planned, I returned to work on Monday, October 17th. It felt so good to re-enter the working world. Everyone at my office provided me with positive thoughts and welcomed me back. Mid-morning our Vice President of Human Resources came into my office and sat down. "Welcome back. We want you to pace yourself. Don't over do it. I know you want to jump back in at 110% but please take it easy. I spoke with our Office Manager and we both agreed you should consider working from home two or three days a week. Especially since half your time is spent on the telephone, creating presentations and sending e-mails."

I felt overwhelmed by their offer. They cared about me and showed me through their actions that my health was more important than how many hours I worked. What a great company! Every day moved closer towards normality.

Tuesday felt like a regular workday until I came home. Andrea looked at me and said, "You look exhausted with big bags under your eyes." Going through the motions of returning to work stole all my energy. My body showed outwardly what I hated to admit. The time it took to shower, get dressed, drive to work, attend meetings, return e-mails, find new business opportunities and finally drive home zapped all of my energy.

We ate dinner as a family. I cherished our time at the dinner table. Sydney and Jacob always asked me, "Dad, give me a math problem." Andrea and I always giggled at their tenacity. The kids made me proud of their inquisitive and razor sharp minds.

After dinner the phone rang. The caller ID showed my brother Steve's cell phone. He was awesome about checking up on me and asking how I felt. "David, it's Steve. You won't believe what happened today. A police officer came to our door. Apparently they found our address and phone number in dad's apartment. He didn't show up for his doctor appointment yesterday and his doctor's office got worried and called the police. The office manager at his apartment complex let the police into his apartment. They found him dead in his bathroom."

Oh my God. This was unbelievable. I just talked to him on Friday night. I knew he had not been feeling well and spent several days in the hospital. He needed blood transfusions because of some issue with his spleen. He chewed me out because no one told him I had been in the hospital for nineteen days. He had his own battle to fight so I did not want to bother him. I told him the story of my visualization work on the area where my port was located - how it healed in half the time expected by the nurses and doctors. Then I said to him, "Dad, I created that. If I can make myself heal faster, I'm going to walk again using the same visualization work. I'll be walking again by the time you visit us for your birthday in December." I could feel him smiling. "OK. I'm going to hold you to it. That will be a great birthday present!"

Surreal. Unbelievable. Total shock. My stomach tightened as I drove my scooter into our office. I felt nauseous with tears in the corners of my eyes. "Steve, we need to call Mike and tell him what's going on. Where's dad's body? We need to call Rabbi Shook and find out when we can hold the funeral." My mind raced with emotions. Sadness, anger, and disbelief all filled my thoughts. Thankfully my cell phone had three way conference call capabilities with my brothers on the line. Then the negotiations began. "How quickly can both of you get to St. Louis? What are we going to do with everything in dad's apartment? Are we going to tell mom? What funeral home should we use? How are we going to tell everyone? We need to make sure the coroner's office does not perform an autopsy."

Judaism views the human body as the sanctified receptacle of the soul. Even after the soul has departed, the body must be treated with reverence. Per Jewish law, and under most circumstances, autopsies are forbidden. One exception is where foul play is suspected. An autopsy may be allowed in order to aid the police in their investigation.

We determined Dad's funeral would be held on Thursday afternoon. It felt like "deal mode" during an M&A transaction. So many things needed to be coordinated. My brothers and I divided up the to-do list. Steve really stepped up and took a lot of responsibility with the funeral home and the Rabbi. It took all of my strength to find a bereavement fare on United Airlines. The stress felt overwhelming. Andrea had to quickly shop for dressy clothes for Jacob and Sydney. Could this be a dream?

Once we arrived at our Temple in St. Louis, I knew this was no dream. People we had not seen in 25 years started to gather in the foyer outside the chapel. A man from the funeral home asked us if we wanted to see Dad's body. I never considered or prepared myself to answer yes. Mike, Steve and I looked at each other and decided we did. My dad's brother Marty spoke with strong conviction. "Make sure you boys really want to do this. Once they open the casket, it will be too late. For the rest of your lives, you will always remember how Allan looked today."

The four of us walked into the chapel and braced ourselves while the man opened the upper half of the casket. He looked so peaceful. The funeral home did a nice job dressing Dad in a nice suit and not applying too much makeup. I thought he looked really good. My mind raced with so many memories. I'll never forget when I told him his hair had more gray in it. "It's not gray, it's blonde." Andrea and I often chuckled about his response.

There weren't any smiles on our faces. I felt overwhelmed with grief. How surreal. I had seen enough. My brothers and I agreed, with the casket still open, not to tell Mom. After fifteen minutes with Dad, we walked ourselves back into the foyer. It began to get very crowded as we all waited for the chapel doors to re-open. Dad had so many friends that wanted to pay their last respects to him. What a humbling sight.

I wheeled my manual wheelchair to the front of the chapel. Once we got settled, people started to come up and kiss me and shake my hand. There were neighbors from across the street, sisters of my deceased Grandma Schmidt, several people from Home Depot Expo where my dad worked, and lots of family and friends. What an appropriate tribute to my dad. The Rabbi spoke of dedication. "Allan lived his life through his kids and grandkids. He always liked to brag about his boys. Most people would have given up long ago based on the deck of cards dealt to him. But even with the dark cloud constantly hanging over him, he visited Delores at the nursing home every day. No if, ands, or buts about it. Sure he felt the world owed him something for this unwelcome sickness in his family. Through all of this adversity, he never once outwardly questioned, why him? All of us should strive to be such a devoted husband, father and friend."

After the service, a few family members came up to me and asked if I planned to visit my mom while in St. Louis. Earlier in the year my mom's doctor told her she had cancer in her liver, lungs and brain. She chain smoked cigarettes constantly during my childhood years. Six years after she received her diagnosis of MS, her doctor informed her she had ovarian cancer. She never showed any fear before the operation. "David, one day at a time." They operated and removed the grapefruit sized tumor and performed a hysterectomy. After her operation, the surgeon told us the cancer had not spread outside the ovaries. He also mentioned when ovarian cancer is caught before it spread outside the ovaries, 90+% survive five years. She blew through that estimate nearly seventeen years later.

Her latest battle with cancer proved to be much more serious. My dad asked my brothers and me our opinions on treatment options. We all agreed that our mom did not deserve to go through the pain and suffering experienced with radiation and/or chemotherapy. Steroids and pain medication would be her treatment protocol. This woman had suffered enough.

Her doctor gave us his best estimate of her remaining time. He told my dad he expected her to live another six to eight months. Hearing this estimate, we drove to St. Louis in July so we could spend some quality time with my mom. I wanted to remember her with good thoughts. She beamed with smiles from ear to ear when Sydney and Jacob entered her room.

"Hello Sydney. Hello Jacob. Hi David and Andrea. Who wants a soda? How about some yummy butter cookies? Kids, would you rather watch TV or color some pictures for my wall?

"Hi mom. Don't worry about them. We all came to hang out and spend time with you. Tell me what you want us to bring you for dinner."

"Steak-n-Shake sounds really good. You know what I like. Don't forget a chocolate shake."

Mom sounded really tired. Her voice cracked a lot. I could tell she needed something. "Mom, what can I get you?"

"David, please ask my nurse to come in for a minute. I need to be turned"

After a nurse's aid came in, she closed Mom's curtain to block our view. Unfortunately, I saw something very disturbing. With all of the pillows off to the opposite side of the bed, my eyes focused on her legs. All I could see was skin and bones. That scene reminded me of a feeble prisoner in a concentration camp. I thought to myself, "I can never let this happen to me."

At the end of our visit, we all got very quiet. My mom started to cry. She knew this would be the last time she ever saw us. It drove us all to tears. I cried on the inside. I had not yet learned how to release my emotions on the outside. All I could say as I backed my scooter out of her room was, "Mom, I really love you a lot. We all love you."

After dad's funeral, we all decided to meet at his apartment. Rather than rush to vacate and throw away all of his material possessions, we decided to wait until we came back for Mom's funeral. We looked around and started to determine who wanted the various items my dad accumulated over his lifetime. There were lots of pictures of mom and dad pre-kids. Their wedding album and albums filled with our baby pictures consumed our attention. Once again, another surreal moment as we mentally put post-it notes on dad's stuff. Unfortunately, we knew we would return sometime in the next thirty days.

We flew home on Sunday afternoon. How do you respond to someone when they say they're sorry for your loss? I felt so sad. I lost one of my best friends. We discussed topics where he knew the answers or had an opinion based on his experiences faced by my mom. I had a void in my life and felt numb with anger. How could this happen? Dad should not have died from what we thought to be a ruptured spleen. During our phone conversation the previous Friday, he bragged about the doctor who would perform his surgery to remove his spleen. In his opinion, this doctor had the best credentials in the Midwest for this surgery. "I unfortunately have to wait until he returns to the hospital in three weeks." Why did it have to be this doctor? How complicated could it be to remove someone's spleen?

I returned to work on Monday. Our sales team always met on Monday mornings to discuss our prospects and the likelihood of closing a corporate insurance program within the next thirty days. All of my colleagues shared their sadness of my loss. It really helped to be at work and keep me distracted from wallowing in my sadness. Luckily the day ended quickly after returning phone calls and reading and responding to several hundred e-mails. Numbness overtook my thoughts and feelings.

After dinner, Mike called me. "You're not going to believe this, but mom passed away a few minutes ago. I know we talked about preparing for her death, but I never thought she would pass eight days after dad." Once again we connected with Steven and decided to hold her funeral on Wednesday. All I could think about was how she knew dad had passed away and she wanted to lay next to him. On some level of spirituality, she had to know. None of us told her about dad's death because of her unconsciousness. She knew.

During mom's funeral, the Rabbi asked Mike to stand up and read a letter written by one of mom's dearest friends who had it published in the August issue of the St. Louis Jewish Light:

A TRIBUTE TO DELORES SLOAN...
ON THE OCCASIONS OF HER 70TH BIRTHDAY AND HER
50TH WEDDING ANNIVERSARY

"Visiting with Delores is always a pleasure...talking about old friends, catching up on family happenings and discussing sports and current events. She is so full of life and so excited to share news that you forget where you are...and where you are is either sitting on the edge of her bed or in an adjacent chair in the nursing home where she has resided for over 13 years. Delores has multiple sclerosis, but you never hear her complain. She lets you know, time and again, that she feels lucky. "There are lots of people who would be happy to be in my place," she says. "I can see, I can hear and I have family and friends that love me and come to visit me. And, besides, who would want to visit a grouch...someone who cries and complains. I certainly wouldn't."

Before MS took its toll on her body, she was a tireless volunteer at her temple, Temple Israel. Whether it was planning sisterhood luncheons, preparing for an Oneg Shabbat or attending to altar floral arrangements, she loved being a part of the temple activities. She and her husband Allan were regular attendees at Friday night services and, through the years, Delores developed a warm relationship with Rabbi Alvin Rubin. That relationship has continued throughout Delores' nursing home stay. Rabbi Rubin has let it be known to her family and friends, when they have passed him in the nursing room halls, that she has been a true inspiration to him. And, his esteem for her has been evident through the regular visits he has made to her bedside over the years.

On September 3rd Delores will turn 70 years young. Her friends and family will give her a birthday party as they do every year. She always resists everyone making such a fuss over her. And, on September 11 she and her husband will celebrate their 50th wedding anniversary. Rarely a day goes by when he misses a visit with her.

We wanted to do something special to celebrate these two important times in her life. We wanted to let as many people as we could know what an inspiration Delores has been to us all. We knew "The Jewish Light" had become a touchstone for her and the world she had left behind. We knew that finding our tribute to her in the "Light" would make her feel happy and proud. That was our mission.

Delores may remind us over and over again that she is lucky, but really, we are the lucky ones. We are the ones that have had the privilege of a friendship with a true heroine!"

Hearing those words did it. I broke down and cried. No longer would I be able to speak with the inspiration of my life that gave me strength every day to keep fighting. How sad. I felt a huge void in my life and an even bigger hole in my stomach. I ached inside and out. On our drive home to Colorado from St. Louis, Andrea suggested I call Patti Conklin and ask her for some words of advice. "How do I how to fill the hole in my stomach from the deaths of my dad and mom?"

Patti suggested I find shape and color of the feeling in my stomach. "You need to mourn. Create a journal of the "good feelings" of memories with your mom and dad."

Soon after we parked my van in our garage and unpacked the car, I found my journal and started to write down the good memories of my parents. What made me smile when I thought of them?

While initially mad at my mom for giving away the Thanksgiving leftovers during Andrea's first visit to St. Louis, I smiled as I looked back at the memory. Yes, I missed eating the food during subsequent days. In the big schism of life, her actions seemed very small and insignificant.

While working in Dallas as an investment banker, I joined an adjunct committee for UT Austin's Petroleum Engineering Department. They wanted to explore revising their curriculum to include finance and accounting classes. I brought a younger, biased perspective since I obtained my MBA and used these courses on a daily basis in my current job. My efforts and input were well rewarded. They invited me to give the closing remarks at UT Austin's College of Engineering Spring 1995 commencement. What a cool experience speaking in front of over 5,000 people at the Frank Erwin Center. I felt so proud that my dad could see me on stage and meet the upper echelon of the College of Engineering.

In high school, my best friend, Bill Greenblatt, often joined my family for dinner whenever my mom made her famous spaghetti and meatballs. The two of us easily consumed over one-pound of meatballs by ourselves. I can still smell the sauce and taste the bite-sized morsels.

My mom and dad loved to entertain. They had a monthly supper club that rotated among their closest high school and college friends. Whenever the "Club" rotated to our house, my mom always made an ice cream pie. I loved to help her make this delicacy. She crushed Oreo cookies mixed with lots of butter for the crust that she patted into a thin layer. Baskin Robbins provided the chocolate chip ice cream. On top, my mom created a runny homemade fudge mixture that froze on top. I loved eating the leftovers!

Once we moved to Denver, my dad always wanted to visit us in the summertime. He scheduled his trips to coincide with the Cherry Creek Arts Festival. Several years before, I lost my first job out of college as a drilling engineer with Amoco when oil prices fell to $9.86 per barrel. I took my severance money and bought a round trip open-ended ticket to Paris along with BritRail and Eurail train passes. I traveled by myself with a backpack on my shoulders and no formal itinerary. At several train stations, I met fellow backpackers and asked where they were headed. Without a second thought, I joined them on their adventure. These months proved to be mind expanding. I learned a lot about myself – especially with regard to art. I found Impressionism and abstract art to be fascinating. The creativity and colors opened doors in my mind that led me beyond numbers and formulas. Now I had something else in common with my dad. We always found time to visit museums and the Cherry Creek Art Festival. Andrea and I also began collecting art that helped remind us of our vacation destinations.

Before our wedding, Andrea and I discussed religion. I came from a Jewish background and Andrea grew up in an Italian Catholic household. It was important to me to raise my future kids within the Jewish tradition for a number of reasons. I wanted my kids to experience the traditions of Judaism. Examples included the high holidays and bat/bar mitzvah ceremonies when children obtained their thirteenth birthdays. Being Jewish also meant living as a minority. This lifestyle, in my opinion, helped kids to empathize with other minorities. I could not give up my heritage and tried to impress the importance of these reasons to Andrea. She told me to consider it done.

When Sydney and Jacob were born, we participated in one of the Jewish traditions at birth. For both kids, Rabbi Rubin met at my mom's nursing home where he held a brief ceremony and provided them with their Jewish names. Family and friends witnessed these events. I felt so proud that my mom and dad could be a part of this birthright.

My dad set a very good example for me. He came to all of my football games when I started to play in the eighth grade. It did not matter whether we played a home or away game. He showed up. Looking back, I cherished his showing interest in these games. I now have an excellent reference point for being there for my kids – whatever the activity.

In July of 2005, my dad came to Denver for his yearly visit for the Cherry Creek Arts Festival. Coincidentally, our cul-de-sac held our annual July 4th outdoor barbeque to celebrate the national holiday. We felt so blessed that we lived in a cul-de-sac where all of the neighbors enjoyed each other's company. As we sat at our table and munched on appetizers, something bizarre happened. My dad sat between Andrea and me. As he stuffed his face with hot wings, he needed a napkin to wipe his hands and face covered in barbeque sauce. Andrea wore a casual summertime blouse with a white cotton jacket wrapped around her waist. Andrea snapped at my dad, "What do you think you're doing?" He had invaded her personal space thinking her white wrap looked like a napkin. I smiled and shook my head in disbelief.

How do you wake up with a smile on your face every day while you lay in a nursing home bed? My mom provided me with a stellar example of how to live life faced with adversity. If anyone had the right to complain, she did. Instead of being mad at the world, she looked forward to every day with a positive attitude. To this day, she inspires me to think positive and create reasons for things to get better.

In 6th grade, my music teacher approached me with an opportunity. "We want to produce a musical about Tom Sawyer's life for parents and other schools in our district to enjoy. Your personality fits perfect for the leading role of Tom Sawyer. What do you think?" Too naïve to realize the level of commitment, I graciously accepted. The play turned into a huge success. Several schools from our district attended daytime performances. We also performed many evening shows for family and friends. A number of local newspapers took pictures and wrote stories about our show. My parents were so proud of me!

Every Friday night, my Grandma and Grandpa Schmidt (my mom's parents) had everyone from her immediate family over to their apartment for dinner. These Shabbat dinners included her three children and nine grandchildren. I can still smell and taste the split pea or thick vegetable soup with short ribs, kosher veal chops, and hash brown potatoes that included the burnt scrapings off the bottom of the pan. Although my Grandma always hired help for these weekly dinners, she never left the kitchen the entire meal. "David, eat some more. You haven't eaten enough yet."

Sydney's birth provided my dad with a very special gleam in his eyes. He had one brother. My mom and dad had three boys. My older brother Mike and sister-in-law Linda had two boys. Sydney gave him the little girl he always wanted. Until her birth, I never heard him say, "I love you" or "Pa-Pa loves you". Everything changed with Sydney's birth. She proved to be the catalyst that opened up the sensitive side of my dad. How cool. He would do anything for her.

All of these memories flowed onto the paper in my journal with very little effort. These events all brought smiles to my face and tears of joy in my eyes. Amazingly, the hole in my stomach and the pain of sadness throughout my body lessened. Once again, Patti led me through a painful, traumatic experience and provided me with reasons to feel good about my relationship with my parents.

14

YOU DESERVE IT

The next several weeks proved to be challenging. I went to work every day but only completed the minimum tasks necessary to call myself employed. Everyone at work told me they were so sorry and offered his or her condolences. Two parents dying within eight days of each other caused everyone to shake their heads in disbelief. "You should take some time off from work." I told everyone, "That's not an option. I've had enough time away from work from my hospital stay and rehabilitation process. I really need to work." The presence of people at work prevented me from dwelling on the last two weeks. While the mental pain and anguish from the hole in my stomach disappeared, I walked around in a fog of mourning. I needed to reach down inside myself and grab some of my mom's stellar attitude.

While in St. Louis for my mom's funeral, Andrea and I invited Steve, Suzanne and their two kids to join us in Denver for Thanksgiving. We all needed to be around family and friends after these traumatic events. They agreed to join us and drove from Dallas for the four-day weekend. Kirk, Sandy and their two kids also came for the feast. Kirk brought his deep fryer. The noise and commotion from six kids helped ease our pain.

We had so much fun. The Denver Broncos played the Dallas Cowboys for the late afternoon Thanksgiving Day game. Steve and Sandy rooted for the Cowboys since Steve lived in Dallas and Sandy grew up there. Everyone yelled and screamed at the TV. I enjoyed being the Devil's Advocate in the crowd and coaxing the Broncos to victory. During halftime, Kirk fired up the deep fryer on my driveway. As the five gallons of cooking oil warmed up, the fryer started to spit hot oil on the cardboard liner placed between the cooker and my driveway. Kirk inserted the metal hanger inside the first of two turkeys. The first one had Cajun spices injected into several places inside the bird. The second had minimal spices so as not to overwhelm the kids' pallets. Turkeys that cooked in an oven took anywhere from 3 to 5 hours depending on their weight. Deep-frying each turkey took less than 60 minutes per bird. As Kirk hung the first turkey inside the fryer, the oil reacted with the moisture inside the bird. The oil boiled over the edges and spilled onto the cardboard. I took a deep breath and sighed, knowing the oil would soak through the cardboard onto my concrete driveway. Oh well!

Our feast proved to be better than expected. Kirk and I ate second and third helpings of the entire meal. Thankfully I wore expandable sweat pants since my belly grew outward with each plate of food. After we finally pushed away from the dining room table, Andrea instructed everyone to save room for dessert. "Finish watching the second half of the game. Don't forget we have pecan, pumpkin and chocolate satin pies from Marie Callender's." Sydney, Jacob, Ben, Samantha, Dylan and Emma ran downstairs and bounced off the walls to work off their dinners.

In the morning, Emma started fussing so Steve took her downstairs for a nap. Just before lunch, we took all the leftovers out of the refrigerator for a repeat performance of our previous day's turkey, stuffing and side dish eat-a-thon. Suzanne left the kitchen because her cell phone started ringing. After the call, she came back into the kitchen. "Where's Steve? That was my friend Ahnee on the phone and she heard Steve's name called on the radio. He has thirty minutes to call the radio station to win $100 and register for some grand prize."

Ten minutes later, Steve bolted up our basement stairs. "That was amazing. We have a sports radio station in Dallas called 103.3 FM ESPN. They have this contest I entered where if they pick your name, you have thirty minutes to call them back. If you do so within the allotted time, you win $100 and are registered for the grand prize. Get this. If you win, they send you and a friend on all expense paid trips to the Rose Bowl, Super Bowl, Pro Bowl and a Cowboys game. They pick you up in a limousine for the Cowboys game and you get to watch the game from one of their suites. That would be sweet!"

Two weeks passed. While at my office, my phone rang and startled me. I hadn't placed many outgoing sales calls that day so when my phone rang it took me by surprise. I found myself looking out my window at Longs Peak while I daydreamed and reflected on the events over the last 60 days. My attitude wavered as I thought about how much I missed my parents. "David, it's Steve. You won't believe it. Dude, I won the contest. Since you attended UT Austin, I want you to come with me for the Rose Bowl." Unbelievable. Never in my wildest dreams would I ever imagine Steve would win the contest. I actually forgot he entered. Over the next several weeks, I retold this success story dozens of times.

Until we boarded the airplane from Denver to Burbank, CA, I doubted the radio station would come through with airline tickets, hotel and tickets to the game. Could this really be true? Steve looked me in my eyes and said, "I told you this would happen for real. One of my friends called me after he heard I won. He said with everything that happened with your mom and dad, you deserve it."

My excitement masked my worries. Traveling was hard on my body. How would I get around? Should I bring my scooter or manual wheelchair? What about the football tickets? I needed handicap accessible seats since I could not climb steps. What if I have to go to the bathroom while on the airplane? Without a cane or anyway to make my way to the bathroom I could be in big trouble if I really had to urinate. My internal anger overcame my excitement. Being disabled was such a hassle. Most people took for granted everyday items like taking a shower, getting dressed, traveling in a rental car, or attending sporting events. I quickly spoke back to the fearful voice in the back of my head. "Get over it. You're going to the Rose Bowl to watch your alma mater compete for the National Championship!"

Our flight arrived approximately 60 minutes late, around 11:00 PM PST. My first concern was whether my scooter made it on our flight. I looked out our window and saw the baggage handlers off loading the scooter. My next worry concerned the ramp we checked on the flight as baggage. Without the ramp, we had no way of getting the scooter in and out of our rental car. Did it make the flight? After everyone exited the plane, two men came onto our plane with an aisle chair. I transferred onto the chair and the two men strapped me in tight and wheeled me up the aisle. Normally my scooter would be waiting for me directly off the plane. At this airport, they used a wheel-up stairway for passengers to exit down the stairs. The two men assisting me took me out the door where the concession trucks loaded supplies. I enjoyed the "carnival ride" from the airplane to ground level. My scooter waited for me on the tarmac when the concession truck reached ground level. We picked up our luggage and my ramp but found no one at the rental car counter. They must have closed before our arrival at 11:00 PM. Lovely! Steve sprinted to another rental car company and reserved their last minivan. We wandered in the dark until we finally found the rental car lot and our car. I almost drove off a curb while we craned our necks looking for the car. Our last worries were getting me into the front seat of the minivan, unfolding the ramp, figuring out how to fold down the second row seats, and driving the scooter up the ramp and into the back of the van. Steve did a great job. By this time we both needed a cocktail!

After leaving the airport grounds, we navigated our way to our hotel. I had never driven in the Los Angeles area and nighttime proved to be a challenge as I read Steve's MapQuest directions. Forty-five minutes later, we pulled into the parking lot of a hotel/casino approximately thirty minutes south of Pasadena. We had made it. Steve off loaded my scooter in front of the hotel with our luggage. I waited at the outside entrance while Steve parked the car. It felt like New York City. There were lots of people coming in and out of the facility speaking different languages. They all smoked cigarettes.

After Steve checked in, we found the elevators, fumbled our way to the room and debated what to do next. I felt exhausted from the plane and car excursions; Steve wanted to gamble. He had way too much energy for me. We split up. Steve went downstairs to gamble while I channel surfed on the TV. I needed to decompress and rest before our big day the next day.

Game day. We showered, ate breakfast and loaded up wearing our burnt orange tee shirts. Everyone warned us about Los Angeles traffic, especially driving towards the Rose Bowl. We expected to spend two hours in the car fighting traffic. But it only took forty-five minutes. Once we parked the car, our first task of the day was to exchange our seats for handicap accessible seats. Both Steve and I called the facility weeks before, worried about the issue. They told us it would not be a problem. We fantasized about exchanging our corner end zone seats for 50-yard line tickets. Once the gates opened at 2:00 PM, we walked to the Will Call gate and made the exchange. While our new seats were lower, the Rose Bowl rules said they had to exchange our tickets in close proximity to the section of our original seats – oh well!

Now it was time to party. Steve's Rose Bowl package included free tickets to the ESPN outdoor tent. By 2:00 PM, there were already thousands of UT and USC fans drinking beer and shouting at each other. We waited in line to have our picture taken with the Rose Bowl National Championship trophy. Steve and I patiently people watched as we worked our way behind the trophy. I swiveled my seat facing towards the trophy and cautiously stood up from my scooter seat. I used my right hand to brace myself so I didn't tip over onto the crystal glass trophy. We both proudly raised our left hands with our index and pinkie fingers pointed in the air for the Hook 'em Horns hand gesture. What a classic picture this would prove to be!

Around 4:00 PM we decided to make our way to the football stadium. Before finding our seats, we milled around the various vendors who sold Rose Bowl tee shirts, sweat shirts and other collectable items. After purchasing some must have items, we found our seats. The stadium started to fill with fans from both schools. Within sixty minutes, more that 75% of the 94,000 fans clogged the areas inside the stadium. I had to make a big decision. I needed to use the restroom. Do I wait for the game to begin and potentially miss a big play, or do I go before the game begins and potentially miss the opening festivities? My common sense told me to go before the beginning of the game.

When I left our seats to find the bathroom, swarms of people walked up the entrance ramps towards each section. What I did not realize was the security personnel would close off each entrance when the opening ceremonies began. I tried to make my way back to our seats and ran into a wall of thousands of people who were stopped from going any further. This was not good. Fortunately for me, a few college students attempted to part the sea of people yelling "make room for the handicap guy going back to his seat." I followed the outer wall of the entrance ramp and almost tipped over. I ran over several feet. While shifting my weight to act like a counterbalance, I finally saw the football field. Several Air Force jets buzzed the stadium as three men wearing parachutes glided their way onto the field. I made it back just before the 5:26 PM kickoff!

The next four hours proved to be the best National Championship college football game ever witnessed by fans across the country. What an offensive performance by both teams. With 6:42 remaining in the game, USC led the Horns, 38 to 26. I looked at Steve. "This game is not over. This is the Vince Young show." Over the next 2:39, Texas took the ball 69 yards and scored a touchdown and extra point to make the score 38 to 33. Our seats were in the corner of the end zone near USC's band. It was so cool watching Vince Young run the football seventeen yards directly towards our seats. USC took the kickoff and started moving the ball. Neither team could stop the other team's offense. On fourth down with two yards needed for a first down, USC tried to run the ball. Denied! Texas took the ball over with 2:09 remaining on the clock and needing fifty-four yards and six points to win the game. With only thirty seconds left, Vince Young ran the ball eight yards for another touchdown and completed the two-point conversion. I jumped out of my scooter with my hands high in the air. Touchdown! Texas now led 41 to 38 and denied USC's last efforts since they had no timeouts left. Unbelievable; we won!

The crowd erupted with overwhelming joy. Confetti flew everywhere. We stayed in our seats and watched Texas being awarded the National Championship trophy. Vince Young also accepted the MVP award. This game would be the main topic of discussion for weeks after I returned to Denver. All of the issues that consumed me with worry about traveling to this event melted away with tears of joy. The time we spent in California at the Rose Bowl was a lifetime experience never to be forgotten. Steve and I will always remember our time together at that incredible game.

15

THE SKY IS FALLING – PART II

What a game. What a story. I told everyone about our trip for weeks after I returned to Denver. Every Wednesday after work, I resumed my Pilates class at HeathSouth. Life appeared to return to normal until three weeks after the game. While at Pilates, something didn't feel right. My energy level felt very low and I had no power in my legs for bridges while lying on the mat. I almost fell while transferring from my scooter to the trap table. My mind raced through my memories as I tried to determine what could be wrong. I did not want to admit to Andrea my initial personal diagnosis. What changed? Could my weakness be attributed to another exacerbation?

Any adult male would likely admit they did not like seeing doctors. I was no different. "I'll feel better tomorrow," I kept telling myself. Over the next several days, I kept hoping tomorrow would be better. Much to my disappointment, every day got worse. Several times over the weekend I crashed to the floor. It took all of my energy to reach all fours before awkwardly transferring to my scooter seat. What a frustrating experience. Cuss words flew out of my mouth. Not again!

The accumulated stress on my body must have climaxed into an exacerbation. While drinking my morning cup of coffee at work, I reflected back to reasons for my current nightmare. First, I spent nineteen days in the hospital after a blood infection turned septic. Second, I completed comprehensive physical and occupational therapies at home for three weeks after my extended hospital stay. Third, after finally returning to work, both of my parents died within eight days of each other. One trip by plane and another by car to St. Louis consumed all of my energy. Fourth, the stress from traveling to and from the Rose Bowl game awakened my disease in the form of an attack – a very serious attack. All of this occurred within a five-month period. A second exacerbation within six months seemed unreal. Why me? Why now?

I finally scheduled an appointment with my neurologist's Nurse Practitioner on Wednesday afternoon. We met right after lunch so I could still return to work for a few hours after the appointment. Regardless of how I felt, I did not want to miss any more work than was absolutely necessary. Guilt consumed me for always taking time away from my job to attend doctor appointments.

Rae called my name. She brought me back to a treatment room and asked me the purpose of my visit. A wave of desperation came out of my mouth as I described my condition to Rae. "Something is really wrong. I've felt poorly for over a week and finally decided to see you. The left side of my body is screwed up – I can't lift my left leg at all. I really feel bad. My energy level is extremely low. Something has happened to my left arm. I've lost about 50% of its function. I cannot lift my left arm over my head anymore. I'm really scared since I'm left handed." During my previous attacks, I always felt confident I could rebound close to my prior level of activity. Not this time. All I could think about was lying in a nursing home bed like my mom. I felt helpless. I really wanted to cry but no tears came out of my eyes. Where was this tour bus taking me?

Rae left the treatment room for a few minutes and paged Dr. Corboy. I overheard her describing my symptoms to the doctor. "John, he is really scared this time. He must be having a major attack." When she came back to my room, Rae told me Dr. Corboy wanted me to schedule a MRI for the next morning and immediately began five days of IV steroids.

I cringed at the thought of another round of steroids. My history with this treatment was not good. Exacerbations are usually treated with a high-dose, short-term course of powerful steroids. The goals of this treatment should be to reduce the severity and duration of the relapse by decreasing inflammation, and potentially minimizing any permanent damage resulting from the attack. My experience with IV steroid therapy showed limited reduction of symptoms. I never fully rebounded to my pre-exacerbation level of activity. Every time I needed the infusions, I spent many nighttime hours counting the raised texture bumps on my ceiling. Even with sleeping pills I still could not sleep more than two or three hours. Late night TV became my best friend when I finally arose from bed after frustrating sleeplessness. I also learned steroid use can increase a person's risk of developing osteoporosis. Wonderful. Another possible disease caused by treatments to my existing chronic condition.

Dr. Corboy's team once again delivered timely treatment. Within an hour of returning to work, a homecare nurse called me and said her company received insurance company approval for five days of steroid infusions. She asked me what time I wanted to begin after work. We scheduled the visit for 7:30 PM. Shortly after I hung up the phone, it rang again. The MRI Department from the University of Colorado asked what time to schedule my test on the following day. "Let's do it at 8:00 AM so I won't miss too much work."

The homecare nurse arrived a few minutes early so we could attack the stack of paperwork required by her company. I sounded like a broken record to myself. Every time I needed steroids, I had to recant my medical history, medications, doses of each medicine, and family medical history. Now it was time to insert the IV needle. How many tries would it take? I did not want to psyche out the nurse with my history of having difficult and hard to find veins so I kept my mouth shut. She did a really good job. It only took three attempts. My last round of steroids the previous summer had proved less successful. The homecare nurse had tried six times before I finally asked her to leave and send someone else the following day.

When I arrived for my MRI, the admitting nurse asked me a number of questions. The one question that raised a red flag with her pertained to my implanted intrathecal baclofen pump. They could not perform the MRI before turning off my pump. Apparently the pump could malfunction and over inject medication during the test if it was not turned off. What a hassle. How long would this take? More time away from work – what would my boss say? After finding someone in the Pain Management Department to turn off my pump, they finally called my name for the test. I had to transfer to a wheelchair since they would not allow my scooter in the testing room. After the wheelchair arrived, I had to wait for an extra person to help me transfer since my legs did not want to work at all. Tick, tick, tick – I watched the second and minute hands rotate on the clock in front of me. More time waiting and more time away from my job.

I never liked the sound of the MRI machine. Even with earplugs, the irregular banging noise proved deafening. After thirty minutes of counting to myself trying to pass the time, the technician came into the room and injected me with gadolinium. In people with MS, gadolinium-enhanced MRI activity correlates with disease activity. Three days after the test, Dr. Corboy called and confirmed what I already knew. I had current disease activity with two enhancing lesions that proved my disease had awoken and was wreaking havoc on my body and attitude. He also wanted me to resume interferon shots to try and slow the progression of the disease. I had not taken any interferon for more than a year. While I knew this attack resulted from bottled up stress, I did not want to get any worse. So I reluctantly agreed to live with flu-like symptoms three days a week indefinitely. But more importantly, I faced a monumental dilemma. Could I keep the current pace at work while my disease to continued to progress?

My frustration built during my steroid treatments over the next five days. Self-infusing the medicine proved relatively easy. Twice a day I took a bag of Solu-Medrol steroids out of my refrigerator and placed it in a warm pot of water to bring it to room temperature. After unwinding the infusion tubing, I connected the large mouthed, pointed end of the tubing to one side to the clear bag of medicine. The other end connected to my IV line. After filling the line with medicine and holding the line lower than the bag to remove air bubbles, I connected the tubing to my IV line and hung the bag on a portable extension tripod. The bag hung several feet above me allowing gravity to work to my advantage. One hour later the bag had emptied into my arm. I used an alcohol swab to clean off the connection to my IV line and flushed it with heparin and saline to keep the line in my vein open and ready for its next infusion in the evening.

Outside of the infusions, one daily activity proved challenging and difficult to manage. For forty-five years, I ate meals using my left hand to hold a fork or spoon. This exacerbation limited my range of motion in my left arm to the point where I could not lift my fingers above the top of my shoulder. I also lost significant dexterity. Grabbing pills and holding on to them proved especially challenging. Day after day I took pills out of their bottles and dropped them on their way to my mouth. It also took several attempts at forking a piece of meat before it finally found the proper destination. Too often, my food fell to the floor. My basset hound loved me whenever I dropped food. I finally gave in and fed myself using my right hand. It felt so clumsy but the likelihood of food making its way to my mouth improved with every attempt. Using a knife with a fork proved to be a different story. I cringed as I unsuccessfully learned I needed help. Rather than pick up an uncut piece of meat and eat it like a caveman, I found myself asking Andrea to cut up my food. In many cases, it became easier to scoop up my food with a spoon instead of a fork. While no longer a graceful eater, at least I adapted out of necessity.

After finishing five days of steroid infusions, Dr. Corboy suggested I resume physical therapy. I knew my energy and strength were greatest in the mornings so I scheduled appointments for 7:00 AM. For the next two months, I spent two or three days per week trying to regain my strength. The therapist had me work on strengthening my arms by using a machine where you push and pull your hands clockwise and counter clockwise with resistance for five to ten minutes. I walked with a walker and climbed up and down several steps until my energy evaporated. Yes I felt stronger, but not to my pre-attack levels of strength and endurance. "Don't give up. You have to keep trying," I kept pleading with myself.

Someone once gave me an interesting analogy for people with MS regarding energy. "View your internal energy as a quarter dollar in increments of pennies. You only have twenty-five cents per day so try and spread your energy over the entire day. If one activity takes fifteen cents, you only have ten cents left for the remainder of the day." The physical therapy sessions lasted between forty-five and sixty minutes. Unfortunately, I spent at least fifteen to twenty cents per session so I felt worthless and exhausted at work for the remainder of the day. Once again, I felt guilty for placing my health above work. It bothered me that my priorities seemed mixed up – or were they? My mind played more games of mental gymnastics.

While everyone at work fully supported my efforts, our new national sales leader imposed a rigorous standard for Sales Professionals like me. Marsh required each member of the sales team perform and document fifteen in-person sales calls with prospects and centers-of-influence such as accountants, attorneys and investment bankers. I stared at my computer screen as I read this new edict. How am I going to fulfill this requirement when I only have ten cents of energy after each session of physical therapy? This issue consumed my thoughts. What were more important – work and making money or health and living life?

16

MY SECOND MAJOR DECISION

A song from The Clash kept playing in my mind, "Should I stay or should I go?" Yes, I resumed working. But could I reach my pre-attack and pre-hospitalization levels of strength, energy and productivity? I spent ten cents of energy taking a shower, dressing, and driving to work every day. Any day when I had to load and unload my scooter for one or more sales calls burned another ten to fifteen cents to the point of deficit spending. This could not continue. My body screamed for help while my mind kept pleading not to give up.

I found myself reflecting on the last twenty-one years of working after undergraduate and graduate school. The adjectives that best described me during these years were ambitious, relentless, persistent, Type-A, competitive, tireless, tenacious, motivated, determined, go getting, and creative. After months of fighting to stay upright, focused and positive towards my latest recovery, I found myself thinking the unthinkable. My mind focused on words that never previously crossed my mind. Tentative, discouraged, self-pity, unsure, doubtful, afraid, paranoid, indecisive, confused, beaten down and tired. How could these feelings come from me? Why was I wasting brain space on such negative thoughts? The simple answer - I was lost.

Andrea and I discussed my dilemma. In my heart, I knew things had to change. I could no longer keep my former pace during waking hours. She knew it and I knew it but I could not admit defeat. What were my alternatives? Do I re-enter my company's short-term disability program? I had three months remaining in this program before my disability was categorized as a long-term disability (LTD). What about retiring with a permanent disability? No way. My mind told me this alternative would be equivalent to giving up. I kept seeing myself lying in a nursing home bed like my mom, totally disabled and powerless with no ability to provide for my family. STOP. STOP. STOP! Do I make my decision with my head or my heart? Anger overcame me and climaxed with a phone call from my brother Mike.

"Hey. So how are you feeling? Linda and I have been worried about you and wondered what's been going on?" It's too bad Mike asked those questions. My anger and frustration climaxed before answering his questions. When the phone started ringing, we watched a taped American Idol episode on our DVR. "Mike, hang on a minute while I drive my scooter to the front so Andrea and the kids can watch their show." I held the phone in my left hand and pushed the forward paddle on my scooter. How much I should really tell him? Well, he asked, so I'm going to unbottle my growing discontent. Unfortunately I no longer had the luxury of discussing my feelings with my dad. He always knew my perspective since lived he the nightmare with my mom.

"Well, do you really want to know? I can't believe I'm going to say this, but life really sucks." With every word that came out of my mouth, my voice kept getting louder. "I can no longer lift my left hand over my head, I now have to eat with my right hand, and it takes all my energy to shower, get dressed and drive to work. I am absolutely worn out by the time I get home. Every night after dinner I pass out from exhaustion in my leather chair. I'm not sure I can work any more. How are we going to pay all of our bills?" My tone became less angry and more desperate.

Slow down. I needed to remember that my enemy was MS and not Mike. He started firing questions at me. "Tell me about your company's LTD program. How does the plan define a disability? What does Andrea think you should do? What do you want to do? When are you planning to make a decision? What about working from home? Have you thought about working part time?"

As Mike asked me these questions, I found my mind going somewhere else. Wandering, dreaming, I looked out the tall glass windows on either side of our front door. I heard Mike's questions but felt lonely, afraid and full of disbelief. My dream took me back to Brazil. My group and I walked down the street towards the Casa all dressed head to toe in white clothing. We were in the current room with open palms pointed up and ceiling fans spinning loudly. My palms vibrated from all the positive energy in the room. While in deep meditation, an entity came to me and told me to be true to my heart. "Listen to yourself and you will find the way."

I shook my head and came back to reality. Why am I thinking about walking away from work? Is this a bad dream? When am I going to walk again? How can this be happening to me? Inside my mind I cried with dry tears. How can MS take away my ability to support my family? I instantly realized my working days were numbered. My heart told me my lifestyle needed to change. "Mike, thanks for your call. I've got a lot to think about. Let me do my homework to find answers to your questions. It may take a few weeks, but I will call you back."

After fighting morning traffic and driving from Highlands Ranch to my office downtown, I parked my van in my reserved parking space. While still sitting in my seat, my mind reflected back to the previous summer. Last year I had to swallow another large pill while exiting from the driver seat of my Honda Pilot. My lightweight foldable aluminum walker sat next to me in the front passenger seat. I reached for the walker, pulled it across my body and unfolded it onto the concrete floor. After using my arms to pull each leg from my floorboard to the garage floor, I transferred my weight to the walker. Steadying myself before shifting my weight from side-to-side, I dragged each leg to the back of my car with assistance from the walker. With one hand on the walker, I used the other hand to balance myself on the car before I pulled open the hatchback. I had to duck when the door opened. Unfortunately I lost my balance and fell backward. The walker went flying off to the side of my car as my head made direct contact with the concrete floor. While I never lost consciousness, I did see different colored stars and dots through my eyes. Luckily a man walking towards the P2 elevators saw me fall and sprinted over to me and dropped his briefcase.

"That was a wicked fall. I saw you hit your head. Are you OK?"

All I could do was nod yes. He helped me to my feet and onto my scooter seat. I shook around each body part to make sure there were no broken bones. Only after I told Andrea several days later did I realize my headaches were symptoms of a concussion. As with many of my falls, I let several days pass before admitting to her I fell.

I did not want to worry or bother Andrea with more heartache from watching me personally implode as my disease worsened.

Once Andrea heard about my latest falling episode, she suggested I find an alternative means of transporting my scooter and me. I settled on a full sized Ford E-250 conversion van with a lowered floor and Braun Vangater II lift. The van had hand controls and the driver seat rotated 180 degrees, moved up, down, forward and back, and swiveled, allowing for a much safer transfer to my scooter. Thankfully modern technology improved for people like me who were disabled but wanted to continue living life independently. The price tag was over $38,000. Another problem solved; all it took was money!

My employer helped me solve a problem created by the purchase of the van. Our building's indoor parking garage offered several handicap parking spots on the lower level. The ceiling clearance provided 6'7" of clearance in the lower floors. My van was seven feet tall. Marsh offered free indoor parking to employees with titles of Vice President, Senior Vice President and Managing Director. Assigned parking cost more. When Marsh learned of my new situation, they made an exception and accommodated me with an assigned space on the first level. I felt so fortunate to have an employer who respected me, valued me as an employee and wanted to help make my life easier.

As I exited the elevator onto the 21st floor, I pushed the handicap button that opened the door to our office. Several people walked down the hallway with their morning cups of coffee. "Good morning," I said to several colleagues after the door closed behind me. While driving down the hallway towards the break room, a fellow Sales Professional asked me if I needed help with my coffee. "You are so kind to ask. Sure." It was hard enough negotiating the curved entrance to the break room without holding anything so I welcomed the invitation for help. After placing my cup on my desk, John headed to his office three doors away. I pulled my scooter behind my desk and prepared to transfer to my desk chair. After lifting the lever under my scooter seat, I shifted my body weight, placed my feet on the floor and turned my scooter seat at an angle facing my desk chair. I swiveled the desk chair and positioned it to make the transfer easy. I pushed up on the arms of my scooter seat before putting weight on my legs and rotating my butt towards the desk chair. My arms reached for the desk chair when I started to sit.

Unfortunately, my aim failed me and I plopped onto the floor. Damn it. Another fall to hide from Andrea. No structural damage but I did bruise my ego. I always wondered what the underside of my desk looked like! After several minutes of repositioning my legs and reaching all fours, I placed one hand on my desk and the other on my scooter seat. Thankfully, I had good upper body strength, leveraged myself upward and fell into desk chair when it started to roll. Winded, panting, and yearning for a sip of coffee, I wiped the sweat from my brow and turned on my computer.

After reading and responding to several e-mails, our local Vice President of Human Resources grabbed the doorjamb to my office. She peeked in to see if I was on the telephone. While my hands-free headset to my telephone wrapped and rested around my neck, I said "Hi Laura, come on in."

"I heard you had some difficulties this morning. I wanted to make sure you were OK. If you have a few minutes, let's talk about a few personal issues". She reached around and closed the door to my office. I thought to myself, this must be serious. "Several of us are really concerned about you. I know you are currently working a couple of days a week from home. That makes total sense since you can talk on the phone and write presentations from home without the stress of driving to work so early and getting in and out of your car so often. I'm wondering if you've thought about working part time? We have a few people from our office that find part-time work easier to help manage their lives."

"Well, I appreciate your idea, but earlier this week I spent a few minutes reviewing our employee handbook. Working part-time creates a major problem with the calculation of income if I ever enter Marsh's LTD program. To my knowledge, a person's LTD benefit is based on their annual base salary in effect before they become disabled. If I work part-time, my monthly benefit could be substantially reduced." I paused. "Laura, I can't believe we're even having this conversation. Never in my wildest dreams would the concept of entering our LTD plan ever cross my mind. I really enjoy working. Unfortunately, some things need to change with my existing lifestyle so I guess I should spend some time understanding the plan."

For the first time in my life, I became consumed with the thought of no longer working. Would people think less of me for giving up? Could my family survive financially? What would I do every day? How would I provide myself with mental stimulation? My obsessive-compulsive, Type-A personality engaged in these deliberations with myself. I needed to thoroughly research our LTD program and understand the financial implications of my actions.

On my drive home from work, I rehearsed in my mind what I would say to Andrea. After dinner, I asked her if we could have a serious conversation. "You probably won't be shocked to hear this, but I'm going to spend the next several weeks evaluating our LTD plan and see how it would effect us financially. I need to do my research and create a spreadsheet before I come to any conclusions. You know me too well. Every decision I make follows a process." My engineering education trained me to be methodical and do the math.

There was a long, uncomfortable pause in our conversation. I could see relief in Andrea's eyes. A serious, decisive tone in her voice took me by surprise. "You're not going to hear any argument from me. I'm worried about you a lot. You are trying so hard but you need to take care of yourself. We can make it work."

The next day I started evaluating our LTD program. Thankfully I worked in the risk management and insurance brokerage industry. My on-the-job training taught me that every word in an insurance policy or program had a meaning. That meant I would need to read, reread and ask a lot of questions. Very quickly I learned that local resources, like Laura, would not answer my questions. From a liability perspective, Marsh directed me to ask all of my questions through our Employee Service Center hotline. I must have called the toll-free hotline two or three times daily for several weeks. Many times I called them to confirm the consistency of their previous answers.

What a complicated program. Up until this exhaustive review, I made payroll deductions to pay for most of the company offered benefits – some pre-tax and some with after-tax payroll. Now my family's livelihood depended on my understanding of every word of the program. I could not afford to make any mistakes.

Our handbook described our disability program in four parts. The first part covered a Short Term Disability (STD). While on STD, the program paid 100% of your salary during the first thirteen weeks of absence and 80% of your salary for the next thirteen weeks. My nineteen-day hospitalization and subsequent recovery period had burned through all twenty-six weeks of STD.

What happened after twenty-six weeks? The second part of the plan described the Basic LTD benefit. The Plan provided employees with a monthly benefit of 40% of pre-disability earnings. Marsh provided both the STD and Basic LTD programs as a benefit to employees with no cost to us.

Our company also offered employees the ability to purchase optional coverage under the Optional LTD Plan. This part provided employees with a monthly benefit of 20% of pre-disability earnings. Anyone who chose to purchase this benefit did so with after-tax payroll and therefore any benefits paid would be tax-free. The fourth part of our plan covered income qualified under the LTD Bonus Income Plan. Incentive bonus awards of $5,000 or greater counted and provided a monthly benefit of 60% of the bonus. I had two bonuses that qualified under this program. Since I paid these bi-monthly premiums in after-tax payroll, this benefit would also be tax-free.

After reading and rereading these paragraphs several times, my head began to feel very dizzy. I questioned myself if I really wanted to keep going. It seemed easier to do nothing and keep working. Or did it? The voice in the back of my head spoke up. "Remember why you changed jobs. Subconsciously, you knew this time might come. Admit to yourself that you joined Marsh five years ago because of the disability benefits they offered to employees. While still walking at the time, you knew their LTD program gave you piece-of-mind since you are the provider for your family. You paid for these benefits so why not take advantage of them?"

After shaking my head sideways, I continued reading and digging further. Along each online page in the right margin there were several links to more information. "How the Plan Works" caught my attention. I clicked on "Disability Explanation". The next page described the crux of the entire program.

"What is the Plan's definition of disability? To be considered disabled, you must be "totally" disabled. During the first thirty months of an approved disability, you are considered totally disabled if you are unable to continuously perform the substantial and material duties of your present occupation because of an illness or injury, as long as you are not engaged in any other occupation or employment. Medical certification of disability is required, and you must be under the regular care of a licensed physician who is qualified to treat your condition."

After thirty continuous months of disability payments, the definition changed. A person must be "continuously unable to engage in duties of any substantial gainful employment for which you are reasonably qualified by education, training or experience. "I wasn't worried about being unable to continuously perform my job because I knew physically and mentally I could no longer keep up with my job responsibilities. Dr. Corboy would need to be involved with the paperwork necessary to document what brought me to this stage of my career. I cringed at the amount of paperwork and how long it would take him to complete it.

Certain words in the definition of disability gave me pause where it stated, "as long as you are not engaged in any other occupation or employment." Wow. My new reality caused my heart to skip a beat. I had to retire and could no longer work. It started to become obvious my working days really were numbered.

Another topic in the right margin gave me another reason to pause – "Other Sources of Disability Benefits". In tabular format, the first item listed Social Security. "Your disability benefit will be reduced by the amount of benefits you receive from Social Security disability income. If you are eligible for a Social Security disability benefit but do not apply for it, your long term disability benefits will be reduced by the amount of Social Security benefits you would have been paid if you had applied to Social Security. The offset will be reimbursed if you provide proof from Social Security that your request for benefits has been denied."

In my mind, I underlined how my disability benefit would be reduced by the amount of Social Security benefits whether or not I applied. My first "job" after retiring would be completing the application for Social Security benefits. I called the Social Security Administration's (SSA) 800-phone number to be educated on their process and the amount of benefit available to me. One word described this benefit. Significant. We could not afford to lose the offset amount since Social Security represented 40% of my overall disability benefit.

One day Andrea came home from work and said someone had told her about Social Security disability benefits for children. While I initially dismissed the idea, the SSA confirmed on the phone our kid's eligibility for benefits until their eighteenth birthdays. Once approved for Social Security disability income, our income would increase approximately 14% with benefits for Sydney and Jacob.

On the income side of the equation, I now had a reasonable understanding of the different sources of my disability benefits. We would have five different streams of income:

1. Social Security disability income;

2. LTD benefit less the Social Security offset (40% of pre-disability salary and taxable);

3. Optional LTD benefit (20% of pre-disability salary, non-taxable since I paid with after tax payroll);

4. LTD Bonus Income (non-taxable); and

5. Social Security income for Sydney and Jacob.

The next phase of my analysis drove Andrea crazy. I wanted to know where we spent money and how much we spent on each item per month. The reason for such detail was simple: compare our pre-disability income to post-disability income and see if we had enough money to pay our bills. The interesting part of this analysis revolved around federal and state income taxes. Certain items like dry cleaning or gasoline to and from work would either be eliminated or substantially reduced. Since some of my disability benefits would be tax-free, the end result proved interesting. The after-tax impact of retiring meant I could earn approximately 90% of my take home pay and no longer have to fight the battle of working. I could instead focus on improving the quality of my life through exercise and stress reduction. While surprised at first, I felt relieved at the potential outcome. I took a long breath in and blew out with tremendous force. We could make this work. Andrea's foresight had once again proved to be absolutely correct.

Over the next few days I discussed my conclusions with several colleagues at work. Everyone stared at me with disbelief. Several people said, "This is a no-brainer. Why work when you can earn 90% of your income and focus on improving your health and feeling better?" I kept hoping someone would disagree with me. My mind could not let go and give in to my disease. Looking for a voice of reason, I called one of my very best friends and former business partner in Houston.

"Hey, Mark. Do you have a few minutes? Out of everyone I've spoken to about potentially retiring from work, you have a very unique perspective. You listened and watched my consternation as I debated walking away from investment banking when first diagnosed with MS. I'm lost and need your sense of reason to help me think through my options." I told Mark about my last three weeks of detailed analysis. "Mark, this is the toughest decision I've ever had to make."

Mark had an incredibly sharp mind. We both had petroleum engineering degrees and MBA's. He was an honest, deep thinker with years of sacrifices made by him and his family. He worked late, traveled week after week, missed several events but knew his family stood by his work ethic. I had tremendous respect for his opinion. After a moment of silence, he jumped on my last comment.

"David, wait a minute. This is the easiest decision you've ever made and you're calling me to vet the idea and shoot holes in your analysis. I can't. Your analysis is sound. Let me provide you some perspective. Men feel a unique, triangular sense of responsibility. You want to be a good husband, father and provider. From my perspective, you are an excellent, caring husband and father. The analysis you've just completed proves you can still be the provider to your family. You know how hard I've worked to build my career. Vicky and our two kids have stood by me and knew there would be a lot of missed sporting events, dance recitals and other family functions. I sometimes regret my decisions because I can't go back in time and ask for a do-over. You have the ability to create a legacy with Andrea, Sydney and Jacob. You can be there for them. I'm envious at the relationship you have with your family. It will only get stronger. Get over this mental roadblock you've created. I know you love to work but you can live your life vicariously through me!"

How could I argue with Mark's feelings from within? I needed to disconnect from voice mail, e-mail and overall job responsibilities. I wanted to walk again so I needed to commit to putting my health above work. No second-guessing myself any more. It was time to move on to the next phase in my life's journey. Suddenly I felt mentally stronger and hopeful again. Everything would be OK. While I thought people would try and convince me to stay, everyone I told was very supportive of my decision to disconnect and "retire".

I decided my last day at work would be Friday, April 14th. On Tuesday, I sent blast e-mails to friends, colleagues, prospects and clients: "I wanted to let you know I am "retiring" from Marsh through our long term disability program so I can focus on improving my health. My last day in the office will be Friday, April 14."

Shortly after I sent the message, my computer beeped and let me know I had received a new e-mail. It continued beeping until my last day in the office. I felt humbled by everyone's kind and moving words:

Kim S. (Marsh colleague): "Although we don't know each other very well, I wanted to take the opportunity to wish you life success. It is an important step that you are taking and I hope that you and your family will benefit greatly from your decision. Best wishes to you and your family in your future! I know that you will be missed in Martian land."

Jean (Building management): "Hello, David.... I want to wish you all the very best in your retirement and I hope you enjoy your time with your family to the very maximum. You have been such a pleasure to work with and I can only wish all our tenants at Seventeenth Street Plaza were as considerate as you are. I send you strength and goodwill during your next journey. Thank you for letting our paths cross."

Dave D. (Prospect and friend): "Congratulations and good luck with your health. Your professionalism, manner and personality will be tough for Marsh to replace."

Marty H. (Marsh colleague): "David, though I'm sorry to hear that you are leaving us, I'm very glad that you will be able to focus on your health. Your work ethic, determination and intelligence have been a role model to many. I wish you and your family the best."

Rich V.L. (Prospect): "I wish you luck as you move to this new dimension of your life. You are a terrific guy and I have enjoyed working with you. I know how difficult it has been trying to keep your active schedule and still managing your illness. I have several friends who are in a similar situation and they also made the decision after a time to try and simplify their lives. Your diligence, your high spirit, and your optimistic attitude impress me. We will miss you in the workplace, but wish you well in your retirement. Take care of yourself and do keep in touch along the way. I hope we have the opportunity to cross paths again."

Monte M. (Client): "I wish you the absolutely best of luck in your journey to improved health. Although you have, from time to time, been the "victim" of my expressed frustrations, I want you to know that I have always valued your guidance and advocacy in all of the insurance matters we have placed through Marsh. You set a high standard for those remaining to achieve. I personally will miss your involvement in our business and invite you to stay in touch so that you can continually be kept up to date in this interesting project."

Scot J. (Client): "Best of luck to you and your family, David. Keep up your superior attitude and I know you will handle what you have been given."

Mike T. (Former investment banking employee who worked for me): "Ryan forwarded me your e-mail announcing your retirement. I am aware that you have been fighting some medical issues for a while. You don't know this but I often wonder how you are doing and hoping you are doing well. I hope the time off will allow you to get better and I will keep you in my prayers and pray for your improving health. While I know I have mentioned this to you before, out of everyone at Nesbitt Burns, I have the utmost respect for you and still remember the conversation we had before I left. You were very gracious to me and I much appreciated your words of encouragement. You are the hardest worker I know and I suspect you will likely go crazy during your time off. Take care and if I can ever do anything for you, I am more than happy to oblige."

Wow. These well wishes reassured me that I made the right choice, but only time would tell. My eyes swelled with tears – this time with tears of joy. From now on, I only had two priorities: my health and my family. Nothing else mattered.

17

FAMILY IS EVERYTHING

The day finally came after months of anticipation - our wedding day on April 13, 1991. The skies were dark gray, dreary, ominous and filled with rain. It poured but it didn't matter. We wanted my mom to attend so Andrea and I decided on a small wedding with only our immediate families in St. Louis. My mom rode in a handicap accessible van from her nursing home to the Sheraton Hotel at Westport Plaza. My best friend Bill acted as our photographer to chronicle the day's activities. One of Bill's friends played a baby grand piano as everyone filled the room. Once the piano started playing "Someday" from the West Side Story musical, Andrea began her walk down the aisle with her older brother John. I beamed with joy panning the room trying to smile and acknowledge everyone's presence. My attention quickly refocused on my beautiful bride. What a day; what a woman!

"Please repeat after me," came the words from the Justice of the Peace.

"I, Andrea Jane Germak, take you David Mark Sloan, to be my husband, to have and to hold from this day forward, for better or for worse, for richer, for poorer, in sickness and in health, to love and to cherish; from this day forward until death do us part."

After we both repeated his words he said, "I now pronounce you husband and wife."

At that moment in our lives, neither Andrea nor I truly comprehended the meaning of our vows. We felt invincible. We knew we loved each other. We knew we wanted to spend the rest of our lives together. We really enjoyed each other's companionship. We both liked traveling to exotic destinations to scuba dive and lay on the beach. We both enjoyed art, live music and attending The Jazz

Fest in New Orleans. I knew I found the right woman to marry when she wanted to go tent camping in parks where the only toilet was a hole in the ground. Andrea, in Billy Crystal's words from "When Harry Met Sally", was the epitome of a low maintenance woman - my kind of woman. She never complained, always smiled, had an open mind for trying new things, and cared about people in general and me in particular. Andrea and I each found true soul mates until death do us part.

While we were so excited to marry and spend our lives together, neither of us knew or envisioned the degree to which I would become high maintenance and very needy. Who would have thought Andrea would need to help pick me up after hearing me crash to the floor? Help me cut my food or scoop up the last bite of rice or corn or any food I ate with a spoon? Repeatedly pick up my dropped pills, eating utensils, mail or most anything I held for the briefest of moments? Help me put on my compression socks or dress me for the day? Lift my legs into bed every night? Rearrange my legs in the middle of the night to lessen my pain from violent spasms? Use a Hoyer lift to put me back in my wheelchair when she could no longer lift my deadweight body off the floor? Work every day when I became a stay-at-home dad?

We signed our togetherness contract the day we married. The words "for better or for worse, in sickness and in health" took on a much deeper meaning after my diagnosis. Statistics indicate that a large percentage (approximately 75%) of marriages dealing with chronic illnesses eventually fail. Nobody should have to deal with or care for a spouse in such need. While I worried that my chronic condition dealt Andrea more than she ever imagined, she told me more than once, "Don't worry, I'm not going anywhere." One of my best friend's wives told me, "David, you are so lucky. Andrea is an angel." No one could argue my disease continued to progress. Throughout my living nightmare, Cindy's words provided me comfort that our marriage and love for each other would survive, prevail and flourish regardless of my health. I learned that the definition of love started with one word, commitment. I felt so blessed to have Andrea as my wife.

For the substantial majority of my adult life, the world revolved around me and only me. I lived in a "me" centered world. Sure my world changed after marriage and even more so after the birth of

Sydney and Jacob. My priorities changed for the right reasons. My world now revolved around the three most important people in my universe. But once I learned of my formal diagnosis, one thing bothered me more than any inconvenience, symptom or functionality taken away from me. It devastated me to watch Andrea witness my health deteriorate.

I mentally accepted my disease. Did I like it? Absolutely not, but who wanted to lose their ability to walk? For someone who always needed to be in control, I lost the ability to alter the end result. I changed my diet, exercised more, tried five different FDA approved medications to slow the progression of my disease, and kept a positive attitude. I had to stay strong (both physically and mentally) for Andrea and the kids. While my outward attitude never waned, it frustrated me that Andrea watched me self-destruct. But she helped me stay positive. She listened to me curse when I fell to the floor. She made suggestions after reading or hearing something new on MS. She recommended alternatives to help me become more ergonomic in how I walked with my cane or transferred from our bed to my wheelchair. My life long partner did everything she could just like I did everything I could to fight this miserable disease. Through all of our efforts, my disease continued to progress. I fought back tears on the outside while I cried on the inside. I felt so much pain from my inability to be an able husband, an able father and an able provider.

Beyond this anguish, Andrea gave me strength to keep fighting. We had an enviable relationship. We never fought. There were no reasons to fight. Whenever we had a disagreement, Andrea's perspective and point of view always made sense. The engineer in me listened to her logic while I came to my mental conclusion. Most often, I found myself agreeing with her side of reason. Our symbiotic relationship thrived. She liked to cook, shop, read, care for our children and do things that took patience. I worked long hours in a profession I loved, managed our finances, negotiated with contractors and car dealers, performed yard work, and organized social events with friends, colleagues, clients and prospects. Each of us knew our strengths and weaknesses so our division of labor and interest worked well.

I felt extremely lucky to marry a Registered Nurse who specialized in pediatrics. After reviewing our income and expenses prior to Sydney's birth, we concluded that Andrea should become a stay-at-home mom. Who better to care for our kids? That was an easy decision with an easy answer. Yet Andrea's nursing background also haunted me. After receiving my diagnosis, guilt crept into my mind. I knew it was baseless, but it haunted me that I married a nurse thinking I knew I would need someone to care for me. How could I see into the future? We both knew about my mom's condition, but neither of us knew about my life changing diagnosis for more than seven years after we married.

There were many dark days with dark thoughts after my diagnosis. My mind raced through adjectives like frustrated, angry, overwhelmed and exhausted from worry. I felt embarrassed and paranoid that others considered me disabled. Every time this happened, I reminded myself that I had to focus on what I could do and eliminate thoughts of what I could no longer do. I kept pleading with myself to stay positive. In my darkest days, I asked myself, "Why bother continuing to fight?" It never took long to come out of my personal fog and remember that Andrea, Sydney and Jacob were my life. They gave me strength, they gave me hope and they gave me the singular reason to fight back – my family meant everything to me. Suicide? No way. I enjoyed life too much to take the easy way out. Everybody had his or her own set of problems and nobody wanted anybody else's. In the big scheme of chronic diseases, I knew I could win. I knew I would walk again. I needed Western medical solutions to catch up with my condition and me.

When we moved to Denver from Houston, I was walking without assistive devices. Sydney just turned five and Jacob was three. Watching my needs increase created lots of questions. Daddy, why do you use a cane? Why do you get so tired? Why won't you play in the sun with us? Why do you sit down at the park? Why did we move? Why is one of your shoes wider than the other? Why do you take so much medicine? Do your shots hurt? How many doctors do you have? Are you going to die? Where did that boo-boo come from? We enjoyed them being so inquisitive. Our challenge revolved around providing them answers to every one of their questions at their level of understanding. We never hid anything from them. Our openness with both kids gave me comfort in knowing they always knew about my mysterious disease called MS. They were both so accepting.

When I fell more often and my walking regressed, I began using a scooter to minimize falling. Initially I only used the scooter for long distance walks from my car to my office, to and from appointments downtown, and soccer games. Eventually, my falls became prevalent at home so I needed to bring it inside as well. How would I get the scooter in our house? Online research quickly helped me find ramps to clear our two sets of two steps and our threshold step into our front door. Within twenty fours of ordering the ramps, the provider delivered three ramps to our house. Another problem identified and solved.

When I started bringing my scooter inside, Sydney and Jacob were nine and eight years old. The kids thought a new play toy arrived. They wanted rides on my lap. They wanted to honk its horn. They had few memories of me without needing some form of help with movement. While I cringed at these thoughts, I knew in my heart they didn't care. They wanted their dad to play with them and attend their activities. They wanted their dad to give them math problems. Typical dad stuff expected from kids.

When I asked them for help they never questioned why. "Sydney, can you help me pick up my pill on the floor?" "Jacob, will you please drive my scooter closer to the tub? I fell and need to use it to help me stand up." "Will one of you please call someone in our cul-de-sac? I need help standing up. Ask them to please hurry. I'm stuck on the floor in a weird position and my legs really hurt." Both kids had Andrea's calm disposition so they never appeared distraught or bothered by my constant calls for help. They never once complained. They helped me because their dad needed help. They were good, honest, caring kids with big hearts like their mom.

Our kids provided me with great inspiration and motivation. I wanted to provide them with a positive role model. "Never give up. If you do the best you can, you will never hear me complain." We talked, we laughed, and we enjoyed spending time together. After all, spending more time with my family offered one of the primary reasons to retire. One of the kids once asked, "Dad, do you miss walking?" Sure I did. But my actions needed to show them that walking was only one mode of transportation. Scooters or wheelchairs were no excuse for slowing down. At five to six miles per hour, I could scoot faster than most people could walk.

Sydney and Jacob's hectic lifestyles with after school activities inspired me to get more involved with their lives. I never appreciated Andrea's hectic lifestyle until I lived her life. I always thought,

"What did she do every day?" Not anymore. Instead, I wondered, "When do I get a day off?" I became David's Taxi Service driving the kids to soccer, dance and Hebrew lessons. Yes, I had a disability, but my handicap proved to be more of an inconvenience than a disabler. Since it took longer to get in and out of my car, I had to plan ahead and add a few more minutes to every activity. I would not allow MS to dictate my life. I would not allow my disease to slow me down. My attitude needed to be strong around Andrea and the kids. My actions needed to show them my world revolved around them. They were everything to me. Their actions provided me with a new definition of love - unconditional true love.

Even with kid activities to keep me busy and pre-occupied, my transformation from working every day in the business world to a stay-at-home dad did not come easy to me. I became a work in progress. What would I do all day, every day? I felt like a houseguest. Activities such as cooking, cleaning, laundry, cutting the grass and shopping for groceries all proved too difficult for me to manage or accomplish. The voice in the back of my head barked at me. "Remember to focus on what you can do and not on what you can't do." Enough said. Those words offered great advice to live my life after work.

18

LIFE AFTER WORK

My last day of work was Monday, April 17th, 2006. What a strange day. I packed up my office files, books, and personal belongings and provided background on each prospect in my new business pipeline to our sales team. Normally this occurred when you changed jobs or resigned for a different career. It finally sank in that my disability had forced me to retire. Why did this happen to me? What did I do? Am I really going through with this? Stop now. My workings days were over. While I felt relieved about making the right decision for the right reasons, I also cringed at the thought of walking away from more than twenty years of a successful career working in jobs I loved to do. At that moment, life did not feel fair to me. Then again, how do you define fair? The voice in the back of my head spoke up. "Be happy, you're being paid not to work. It's time to start the next chapter in your life. You should feel very lucky." Unsettled yes. Lucky? Only through the passage of time would I know if I felt lucky.

For my entire career, my life revolved around structure during working hours. I always put aside time for making and returning phone calls, responding to e-mail messages and presenting our capabilities to prospects and clients. But this particular day was different. My last day in the office consisted of saying goodbye to all of my peers. The adjectives that came rushing to my mind were surreal, weird, depressing, exciting, and uncertain. Right after lunch, our receptionist announced to all three floors for everyone available to join me in the main conference room for my last day sendoff. Our office manager, my boss and approximately thirty colleagues joined me for cake and ice cream. People started firing questions at me. "What are you going to do with yourself everyday? When are you going to start writing your book? How does it feel to retire?" All I could do was smile.

My boss made his way to the front of the crowd to say a few words: "What can I say to a guy our office will truly miss. I've never met someone who works harder than David. You would never know he is faced with such adversity by looking at the smile on his face. He has an obvious passion for winning and hates losing. David is a role model for everyone in our office on how to conduct one self with high ethics, honesty, and a superior attitude. Good luck in the rest of your life, my friend!"

Many friends came up to me after the reception and shook my hand. However, one conversation almost made me cry. "David, your attitude inspires me. You never complain. You act very professionally and treat people with a lot of respect. You are such a fighter. You always keep your head down and do your job without getting involved with office politics or gossip. I am amazed that you continued to work for so long faced with your set of challenges. I wish I had your enthusiasm for life! You should know that everyone in the office feels the same way I do about you." Wow. I never knew people felt that way about me. What a cool thing to hear from someone.

The next day I entered my company's LTD program. After breakfast and one cup of coffee I thought to myself, "What am I going to do today?" While there were no guidelines on when to apply, I knew I wanted to immediately begin the application process for Social Security Disability Income – especially with the offset provisions of our LTD program. I read in the Rocky Mountain MS Center's quarterly publication and Inside MS Magazine that some people hired attorneys to help them with the overwhelming paperwork and approval process. Could it really be that bad?

Prior to beginning the online application, I logged into the Social Security website and completed a form called The Medical and Job Worksheet for Adults. Here I summarized my jobs over the last 15 years and listed all my doctors and hospitals attended with dates and patient ID numbers. What a hassle. It took me hours to remember the information they wanted. I also had to call several doctors and hospitals to get their addresses and my patient numbers. What a painful and time consuming activity. I fought through my agony because I wanted to do it right the first time. This collection of information proved to be very helpful in completing the online application. I took me all day to finalize these two documents. What did I get myself into? My head hurt from information overload.

The next day, the website directed me to complete the Adult Disability and Work History Report. This report wanted to know detailed explanations of why I saw each doctor, treatment details, a listing of all my medications and why I took each drug, side effects, and a chronology of every job I held for the last 15 years. For each job, the Social Security Administration (SSA) allowed applicants to write a maximum of 800 words that included details on daily activities. Each of my descriptions used the total allowable words. For each and every essay, I checked the total number of words through the word count function. What an anal thing to do! I spent a total of eleven hours over three days completing the applications and essays.

The local Social Security office informed me by mail it could take as long as 180 days for them to respond with an approval or denial letter. It never crossed my mind that they might deny me benefits. How could they with my fact pattern?

Surprisingly, a letter came in the mail from the SSA after only six weeks. Providing the extra details and comprehensive explanations paid off. The SSA approved my application on the first attempt within six weeks, not six months. What a welcome relief. After receiving my Notice of Award, I scheduled an appointment with the local Social Security office to complete the necessary paperwork for Sydney and Jacob to receive benefits until their eighteenth birthdays. At my meeting, the Social Security caseworker told me that my application and essays were the best she had ever seen. Despite my disability, I still excelled at grabbing a monumental task and using my relentless, tenacious mindset to find success.

It felt good to finish the Social Security process with a positive outcome. My benefits were scheduled to start after the six-month waiting period in October 2006. I attacked the requested information with the same passion of a work project with the potential for contingent compensation. Indirectly it did. So now what? Every day at breakfast, Sydney asked me, "Dad, what are you going to do today?" That question haunted me because I really had no answer. Prior to retiring, my sister-in-law warned me not to over commit myself for the first six months since I had so much free time. "Give it some time to figure out what you really want to do every day. What's important to you today may not be important in six months." Good advice, Linda, but it didn't answer Sydney's question.

What am I going to do today? I thought back to the reasons why I retired from work. Spend more time with my family. Improve my strength through exercise. Slow down and reduce stress. I started with exercise. My first task included time in the swimming pool. This became my Monday activity. I knew I wanted to walk again. The pool offered a way to practice walking with the help of buoyancy. I had to keep my leg muscles strong for when my walking would become reality. Our neighborhood recreation center had a special chair for disabled people to get into and out of the pool. I transferred onto the chair that lowered me into the pool. Without any weight belts, I walked down the middle of the lane up and back. Then I walked sideways up and back. After two laps of each, my legs felt really heavy and I tipped over several times grasping for one of the lane ropes. The voice in the back of my head said, "Don't overwork yourself. You still have to drive home." So true, along with showering and carpool duties. I had to avoid falling to the floor with no one home. Over and over I told myself to slow down. "Pace yourself. There are too many hours left in the day. It's early."

While I only walked a total of one hundred feet, I set a personal goal of increasing my total distance walked by fifty feet each week. Through these efforts, I demonstrated to myself I could walk safely while improving my strength. With the passage of time, I knew I would also be able to do it outside of the pool.

Every Wednesday, I focused on walking with my walker. The biggest hassle of this activity occurred while putting on my tennis shoes. During my rehabilitation process at the hospital the previous year, the physical therapist instructed me to wear my AFOs on both feet when walking because they provided greater ankle stability. It took ten minutes to wrestle them on before my walks. I felt exhausted before I ever started. I measured my progress by how many laps I walked from my bathroom, through the hallway, around my family room and dining room prior to limping back to my bathroom. It took several weeks before I completed one full lap without stops to catch my breath while sitting on the seat of the walker. I had to keep pushing myself because I knew I had to walk again.

Fridays I worked on core strength and flexibility at my Pilates class. We alternated stretching, stomach crunches, and lifting the Fitball over my head and side-to-side. After our mat activities, we spent time on the reformer and trap tables. While not formal exercises, I also burned energy every time I transferred to and from my scooter. By the end of our one-hour sessions, my biggest concern was having enough arm strength to operate the hand controls on my drive home. Working out three days a week every week challenged me to near exhaustion. But I knew in my heart I had no choice. Unless I pushed myself, I could be bedridden like my mom and lose my functionality. No way. That would never happen to me.

My Monday, Wednesday and Friday activities consumed my mornings. What should I do every afternoon? My working days were formerly packed with internal meetings to discuss new business opportunities followed by several prospect presentations. Free time felt weird and unproductive. I made a personal rule never to turn on the television prior to 4:00 PM. That still left me several hours of uncommitted time. Keep it simple stupid! I turned on my stereo and listened to music on the radio. I placed my feet on my ottoman, leaned back, and closed my eyes. For someone with a Type-A personality, I felt guilty for relaxing. Only through the passage of time would I learn to enjoy and cherish my quiet time. My mind slowly decompressed while the layers of stress began to melt away.

Andrea and the kids laughed at me when I told them what I accomplished the following Tuesday. Something so simple yet never crossed my mind. I loaded my scooter into my van and drove to our neighborhood library. Within fifteen minutes, I held a library card in my name. What a concept! I always enjoyed reading spy novels but never made time to read more than a few paragraphs at one sitting in the bathroom. Over the next several months, I consumed several books written by Nelson DeMille and Daniel Silva. It felt good to find a useful activity to exercise my mind.

My transition to a stay-at-home dad felt really good. It felt even better when people asked me what kind of work I did. My answer rolled off my tongue with pride. There weren't many dads who could boast of my current job title. I drove the kids everywhere. I also volunteered in Jacob's math class. My legacy focused on strengthening my relationships with Sydney and Jacob by spending more time with them and being home at the end of every school day.

The month following my retirement, the president of Denver's chapter of Association for Corporate Growth (ACG) invited me to their monthly networking luncheon. Up until my retirement, I had actively participated on ACG's Board of Directors. Once I decided to retire, I resigned my Board seat and membership. I wanted to cut all ties of responsibility to the working world so I could focus on stress reduction and improving my health. Whenever someone asked me about getting involved with ACG, I always recommended finding an area of passion within the service organization. For example, if you liked meeting new people try volunteering for the membership or monthly program committees. In my case, I felt passionate about academia and bettering myself through continuing education.

Since our chapter grew its membership purse, the Board wanted to give back to the community in a meaningful way. We all agreed and authorized a $2,500 per year two-year scholarship for an MBA student. Following the last board meeting of the year, our president asked me to work with the University of Denver's Daniels College of Business to create a scholarship and selection criteria for one of their MBA students. With continued chapter growth, I recommended that the Board create three more scholarships – one for Daniels Executive MBA students and two for similar programs at the University of Colorado. Selfishly, our chapter gained access to brilliant minds and potential new members through these scholarships.

When I arrived at the luncheon, I shook hands and said hi to a number of friends and former Board members. The president ushered me to his table prior to his opening comments. "Before I introduce today's speaker, I want to recognize a friend and fellow Board member. You may have heard that David Sloan retired from the Board and his day job to focus on his health and family. This man contributed tireless hours creating and administering four ACG scholarships awarded to MBA students in our community. We should all learn from his passion in undertaking a thankless endeavor that means so much to our chapter and every student recipient. In recognition of his outstanding efforts, the Board has decided to rename each scholarship the David Sloan ACG Denver Chapter Scholarship. David, your efforts are very much appreciated by all of us. Please accept this plaque from ACG to remind you of your stellar accomplishments."

All two hundred and fifty people in attendance stood up and gave me a standing ovation. I clapped with them. Wow. To hear such recognition from peers gave me goose bumps. I never expected this honor. I did the work because it kept me involved with students, faculty, and premier MBA programs. Everyone acknowledged my efforts in spite of my disability. How cool. I thought you needed to die before an organization named something after you. I guess not. What a pleasant surprise!

With the good, also came the uncomfortable. The hardest part of my transformation related to the role reversal between Andrea and me. Instead of me leaving for work every morning, Andrea left by 7:30 AM every day. Instead of me being stressed out from the pressures of sales and business development, Andrea worked all day and then came home and cooked dinner, cleaned house and washed our clothes. I wanted to help but my disease limited my ability to perform these duties. That sucked and only reinforced my feeling of being a houseguest.

I had to find a way to overcome this feeling of inadequacy. I kept reminding myself to focus on what I could do and not get caught in the trap of only seeing my limitations. What could I do really well? I had a lot of personal experience in career management. I saw people's strengths and how to maximize their potential. I knew Andrea had outstanding nursing skills and great experience behind those skills. She felt overworked and underpaid in her current job. I agreed with her. She deserved better. First, we rewrote her resume. Next, I coaxed her into looking around for another job. Within three weeks of initiating her search, the premier pediatric practice in Denver offered her a great job. I applauded her success. "Way to go, honey. You deserve it. You made it happen!"

Andrea's accomplishment reinforced that I still added value – through coaching others instead of working myself. Many friends asked me if I missed working every day. Good question. Did I miss work? After a long internal debate, I told everyone, "You know, I don't miss the long hours and time away from home. What I do miss are the relationships and social interactions with colleagues and clients." The question only accentuated my internal struggle. I craved using my education, training and expertise to support my family. The unfortunate reality of MS demonstrated my mind sought to write checks my body could not cash.

Shortly after Andrea accepted her new job, I met with Dr. Corboy for my semi-annual neurological exam. We both agreed that my health continued to worsen. How frustrating. Nothing I tried thus far slowed the progression of my disease. I constantly surfed the Internet looking for alternative therapies. The FDA had recently re-approved a medication called Tysabri. This monoclonal antibody proved to be effective in treating the symptoms of MS. Positive outcomes included preventing relapses and significantly improving quality of life in people with MS. It sounded promising to me. But did I qualify for this treatment with secondary progressive MS?

"I've never been so happy to hear someone had an exacerbation. Your attack in late January now qualifies you for Tysabri since you had to have an attack within twelve months of initiating the infusions. Prior to your latest attack, you would not have qualified. Let's hope these monthly infusions help you. We will reevaluate you after one year of treatments to see if it slowed the progression. Stop your Rebif injections immediately since we want that drug to wash out of your system prior to starting Tysabri in September."

Way cool. This drug had to help. My hopes elevated while my mind focused on positive thoughts of walking again. Everyone in the medical profession I spoke to about Tysabri gave me reasons to believe this drug could stop my progression. Only through the passage of time would I know the real answer.

It felt good to have a new plan. I exercised three times per week, relaxed often, and infused Tysabri every four weeks to slow the progression of my disease. Time passed quickly while I stayed busy implementing my plan. After my eighth infusion, I saw Dr. Theriot for my quarterly baclofen pump refill. She told me that driving my scooter caused me to have very poor posture. "When you originally purchased your scooter, you drove it to reduce falling during long walks. Now you drive it full time and sit all day. Your posture is terrible. You slump over when you drive the scooter with your shoulders rolled forward. I want you to go through the approval process for an electric wheelchair. I'll write you a prescription so insurance can hopefully pay for the chair. A properly fitted wheelchair can dramatically improve your posture."

After two long months waiting for my insurance company's approval, the equipment company finally called me with good news. My new chair would be in their store in two weeks. Whenever I started a new medication or converted to a new piece of equipment like my wheelchair, I always had inflated expectations of the benefits.

It never crossed my mind there may be unwanted side effects or needed changes in my daily routine. There were so many benefits to my new wheelchair. Simple things like improved posture, off-road stability for Jacob's soccer games, and the ability to lean back and elevate my feet above my heart to help minimize the edema in my ankles. Unfortunately, the wheelchair wreaked havoc on simple daily activities. Whenever I dropped something while sitting in my scooter, I held onto the tiller handle with one hand while I bent over to pick up the item. With the wheelchair, I had nothing to hold in front of me. On the first night after taking delivery of the chair, I dropped my watch while undressing for bed. I reached down to pick up the watch and went flying out of the chair onto the floor. Oops. It hadn't crossed my mind to grab one of the side arms prior to bending down.

During an average month with my scooter, I fell while transferring or attempting to pick something up two or three times. My time on the floor caused me to make a game out of falling. Like with an alcoholic who counted the number of days since their last drink or a religious person who counted the number of days since their last confession, I counted the number of days since I last fell onto the floor. In the first two days with my new wheelchair, I fell four times. The cuss words flew out of my mouth whenever I fell. "Now I have to start over counting days." Sydney and Jacob always helped me rearrange my body in order to use my upper body to leverage myself back into the wheelchair. "It's OK Dad. No structural damage, right?" They were so helpful and always made me smile about these unfortunate accidents. We all had to laugh even though my safety came into question because it became harder to make my way back into the chair.

"I can't lift you anymore. Your body is dead weight. What are we going to do when a neighbor isn't around to help pick you up?" Once again, Andrea's honesty proved hurtful but true. Enter my worst nightmare.

Two years after I left home for college in Austin, Texas, my mom's primary progressive MS forced her into bed for the majority of every day. My dad moved a hospital bed into our living room to keep her home as long as possible. Whenever I came home during college breaks, I walked through our front door, looked to the right and always found my mom reading the newspaper while lying in bed. Next to her bed sat a Hoyer lift. The shiny metal tubular lift had two octopus looking arms with four metal hooks attached to a canvas sling. With the sling under her body, my dad pumped the hydraulic handle and lifted her out of bed. While she dangled in the air, my dad centered the lift over her wheelchair and lowered her into the chair. MS paralyzed both of her legs and most of her left arm. The disease destroyed them financially while my dad tried to care for her at home. She had to enter the government sponsored Medicaid program and transfer into a nursing home after my dad could no longer provide her the proper medical care at home.

This memory haunted me. When Andrea's frustration grew into a cry for help, I knew the answer. I knew what we needed. The dreaded Hoyer lift would solve the problem. But flashbacks to my mom and her worsening medical condition consumed me with thoughts of the unthinkable. Would my mom's condition become mine? I too lost the use of both legs. I too lost functionality in my left arm. Would we be financially ruined prior to me being placed in a nursing home? No. No. No. I screamed from the inside out. It could not happen to me. It would not happen to me. In no uncertain terms, I told myself no way, no how. I will walk again. I pleaded with myself to stay positive. My hope and attitude drove me back to sensible thoughts. I calmed down because everything became crystal clear. Why else am I always walking in my dreams at night?

19

WHERE NOW?

During the drive to my thirteenth Tysabri infusion in twelve months, I reflected on my health since beginning the infusions last year. Did I feel any better? Not really. My arms felt heavier each hour the day got longer. Heat and humidity still dramatically affected my body by making me really weak. I wilted like a flower when you took it out of water. I could not shower without someone helping me in and out. I needed more help cutting my food and dressing for the day. I fell often during transfers. Nothing in my mind pointed to any improvements. More than once over the last several months, Andrea told me she thought my health regressed further. "You need to stop telling people you're stable because unfortunately you are getting worse." The truth really hurt.

After my infusion, I rode the elevator from the second to the fourth floor for my semi-annual neurological exam with Dr. Corboy. We planned to evaluate the effectiveness of the medication and determine my game plan for the following year. "Mr. Sloan. What can I do for you today?"

"Hi Dr. Corboy. I scheduled this appointment so we could discuss Tysabri and your opinion on whether I should continue the infusions." In my heart, I knew the answer. We discussed the strength in my arms and legs. He asked a lot of questions about the quality of my life. He also wanted to know about any changes in my working status.

"David, you and I have always been very honest with each other. I don't see any signs that Tysabri has slowed the progression of your disease. In my opinion, you should stop the infusions. Unfortunately you've taken five of the six FDA approved medications for patients with MS. While they may have slowed the progression and increased the time between exacerbations early in the life of your disease, nothing has slowed down your disease activity since I've seen you over the last five years. I think it's time to take a break from all of these treatments."

"Wait a minute. You're telling me to stop Tysabri. OK. I cannot disagree with your conclusion. It really has not slowed my progression. I accept that. But what else is out there? What else should I try?"

"I am sorry to tell you but there is nothing else available with conclusive positive results for people in your stage of the disease. Modern medicine has no answer. You are welcome to come back and see me any time you want to discuss your options. I really am sorry."

My chin rested low on my chest after I transferred from my wheelchair to the driver seat. Why me? What options did we need to discuss if I had no remaining alternatives? Why did God pick me to deal with MS and its challenges? I put my car in reverse, backed out of the parking space, and drove home in a heavy mental fog. While merging from I-225 onto I-25 southbound, tears dropped from my eyes. For the first time in my life, I didn't care who saw me cry. No one proved to be more proactive than me. I never wanted to look back over my shoulder and wish I had tried some treatment. Any treatment. This news really hurt – both inside and out. I felt nauseous with despair. How can this be happening to me? No one could compare his or her hope and attitude with mine. I wiped the tears from the corners of my eyes. I breathed in hard and blew out harder. What do I do now? My lips pressed hard against each other. I could not and would not give up hope.

We all sat down for our family meal and discussed everyone's day. Jacob devoured his food since he ran a lot at soccer practice. After eating dinner together, I asked the kids if I could talk to their mom privately for a few minutes. They immediately ran to our office to play on the computer. After telling Andrea the wonderful news from Dr. Corboy, I shook my head in disbelief. "This can't be happening to me. I'm not sure what to do now." It took several days of feeling sorry for myself before I accepted my unfortunate outcome. Every few months I checked online for new experimental drug protocols. There were a lot of trials for people with relapsing remitting forms of MS, but very few for the secondary progressive stage of the disease. There were a larger percentage of people with relapsing remitting MS so drug companies focused on where they had the highest likelihood of making money to offset their large research and development costs. With the passage of time, a wave of desperation hit me hard. The voice in the back of my head screamed at me. "You can't stand by and do nothing. Keep searching."

So I did. One day in early January 2008, I found a protocol for Adult Stem Cell Transplantation for people with relapsing forms of MS. Would I be willing to do this? Dr. Corboy told me about a stem cell transplant study the University of Colorado performed in 2001/2002. Their study had a 4% fatality rate. It seemed pretty high to me. After talking myself into accepting the risks of this treatment to potentially feel better and walk again, I started digging deeper through my own exploratory research. Would I be willing to wipe out my immune system and implant stem cells from a healthy body? Would I be willing to risk death? I debated the risks and rewards with several close friends and family members. My excitement grew after Andrea and I discussed and concluded that I had to try.

Unfortunately, my excitement did not last very long. I did not qualify for any of these studies. First, I had to have an attack within the last twelve months. My last attack occurred two years ago. Each study excluded patients previously treated with Tysabri and/or mitoxantrone. I previously took both drugs. All studies wanted patients who had relapsing forms of the disease and walked. Both answers to these criteria were negative. I could not win. My bravery became overshadowed by my previous aggressive treatments – none of which worked to slow the progression of my disease. Once again, my only option would be to wait for modern medicine to catch up to me. Waiting for others to find solutions proved hard to do, especially for someone who liked to be in control. Sadly, I lost control a long time ago.

Welcome to my world. A world where my hope and attitude exceeded the reality of a chronic disease with limited opportunities to change the outcome. Once again, I learned to accept this unfortunate reality. Not without continued questioning, fighting, and relentless searching for the unfound solution. Yet the time had come for me to back off and live life unburdened for a while. My free time gave me the opportunity to reflect on my decisions since retirement.

One very satisfying decision came after I returned from Brazil. While meditating in the Current Room, the entities gave me the answer to my question, "What should I do that would give me fulfillment?" Soon after I returned to Denver, I implemented their answer. In early 2005, I began my mentoring relationship with the University of Denver's Daniels College of Business. The University's Executive Mentor Program offered me the opportunity to provide MBA students my insights from years of varied work experience. These students challenged me with very thoughtful questions and requests for my opinions. How do you balance your work and personal lives after starting a family? Give us your thoughts on what makes a good presentation. How do you manage a business meeting? Help us with career planning and salary negotiation. What's more important, career progression or job fulfillment?

The ultimate reward came during my second year participating in the program. One of my students worked for an environmental consulting firm. While we dug deeper into her career objectives, I shared with Amanda my background using environmental insurance to facilitate mergers and acquisitions. She became very inquisitive about internships in this industry to help her understand insurance brokerage and risk management for companies with environmental exposures. I introduced her to friends of mine who ran their respective environmental groups at Marsh and IMA. They both provided their perspectives about the industry and career opportunities. I lobbied hard with both companies. Amanda had the background and desire to learn this business. Marsh subsequently offered her an intern position during her final semester. One morning, only weeks away from graduation, my phone rang unexpectedly. It was Amanda. "David. Do you have a few minutes? I am so excited. IMA offered me a permanent position to join their environmental insurance department. This would not have happened without you." I felt Amanda's excitement over the telephone. I could tell she smiled from ear-to-ear while she spoke with elevated syllables of every word. She gave me so much satisfaction. What an amazing accomplishment to help others achieve their goals and dreams!

Recently, I received a very inspiring e-mail from a woman in my third group of students. In our first meeting, I asked each of my five new students what they wanted to accomplish with their MBAs after graduation. Kalyani said she felt trapped with her current employer since they contributed to the cost of her MBA. She did not think it appropriate to leave for a better opportunity since they helped her pay for graduate school. "Wait a minute. You're telling me you can't look for another job until you fulfill their twelve-month waiting period after graduation. Why can't you determine how much your company contributed to your graduate school and negotiate with potential employers so they indirectly repay these expenses? Remember who has control. You do, not your employer. You need to take control of your career and create opportunities for yourself." While in a different context, I shared with the group my experience of IMA paying our moving expenses from Houston to Denver and if I left during my first two years, I had to reimburse them for these expenses. When negotiating with Marsh eighteen months after joining IMA, I shared with them my contractual obligation. In order for me to accept an offer from Marsh, they needed to compensate me for this obligation to IMA. I turned a problem into a solution and watched it work to my advantage.

"Hi David. I just wanted to let you know how much of an impact you made by talking to us about taking control. What you talked about seemed to unlock a whole bunch of routes I can take with my career. Actually, after talking with you, I spent the next three days thinking and weighing possibilities. It's wonderful and feels so free to know how much control I really have. All of this would not have been possible if it weren't for you. You truly made a difference in my thought process! Thank you so much!!! Regards, Kalyani."

Being home every day provided me with many benefits. I liked focusing on exercise and relaxation. I liked spending more time with Sydney and Jacob. I liked mentoring and speaking on behalf of the National MS Society at lunch-n-learn meetings where I helped recruit new teams for the MS Walk and MS 150 Bike Ride programs. I also liked using my free time to look around for investment opportunities.

During the last quarter of 2007, Andrea told me about an available retail space in Highlands Ranch Town Center. We often fantasized about owning a business to complement our rental real estate properties. Andrea always thought owning a chocolate store that also sold red wine would be a big success. Following her enthusiasm, I requested a Uniform Franchise Offering Circular (UFOC) from a Colorado based chocolate company to see if their business model might work in this location. After talking about our next lunch date, my former boss suggested I contact a woman he knew that brokered franchises. Stacy asked me why I liked this company. "Because we love eating chocolate!"

"You need to look beyond what you like and see if this business makes sense economically. If you have time, come see me to discuss companies I work with. Beforehand, take our online survey to help us determine your strengths and weaknesses." Once I completed their questionnaire, we met in Stacy's office. "I remember you told me you were a Type-A personality, but our survey also characterized you as a builder/overachiever." I smiled with a big grin. That description fit me perfectly. Buying one store would not be enough. My personality drove me to think big and create a self-made fiefdom. We talked about some ideas that might work under the absentee owner model: a day spa, haircut salon, mobile storage, and custom picture framing. All of these businesses could be bought under the absentee owner model where I would not need to be involved in day-to-day operations. I could not earn any W-2 income since it would invalidate my LTD income.

After dinner, Andrea and I talked about Stacy's ideas. "I like the picture framing company. It's consistent with our love of art." We looked at their website. Andrea noticed their hours of operation. Her next comment took me completely by surprise. "I might want to work there. I can't see me on my feet all day when I'm a sixty-five year old nurse. They don't open until 10:00 AM so I could stay home longer in the mornings to help you shower and get dressed." How lucky could a man be? What a thoughtful and caring wife. Andrea's words demonstrated our symbiotic relationship. We truly were life long soul mates.

We took the first step in our due diligence. I requested The Great Frame Up's UFOC to learn more. One of their employees called me to make sure we received their information. "I know you are looking to open a new store, but we have a franchisee selling one of their three locations in Littleton, Colorado. Would you be interested?"

Those few words more than piqued my interest. I specialized in mergers and acquisitions in my former life and now had the opportunity to use that skill set to our advantage. Over the next three months, I consumed information about this company. Once we agreed on the acquisition price, I had to write a business plan and arrange bank financing. My obsessive-compulsive personality woke up and put me into "deal mode". I forgot how much of a perfectionist I used to be. I could not sleep. My mind would not shut down.

Andrea forced me to stay away from our computer for an entire weekend. "You need to slow down and take a break." Our efforts proved successful. As of April 1, 2008, we owned a custom picture framing business.

Stress from the acquisition coupled with my disease progression started to cause problems at home. In retrospect, the stress probably created the disease activity. Taking a shower became a major issue. Our shower had glass doors and a four-inch lip to the shower pan. It became very difficult to lift my legs high enough to clear the water barrier of the pan without falling. Andrea would not let me get into or out of the shower without someone's help. Going to bed provided another set of challenges. I could not lift my legs high enough to get into bed at night. I also needed help dressing everyday. My independence continued to slip away from me. In the two-year period since leaving work, I went from showering, dressing, and getting into bed myself to needing help with all of the above. I started losing control. While it took me several years before I learned it was OK to ask for help, I hated depending on others for daily activities most people took for granted.

My feelings were dwarfed in comparison to Andrea's frustration. Several nights while attempting to transfer from my wheelchair to bed, I did not successfully make the transfer. Either my legs stiffened by spasms or they did not carry the weight of my body before I crashed to the floor. Using the Hoyer lift at 10:00 PM was not Andrea's idea of fun. She wanted to sleep and I became an impediment to her rest. I always blamed my falling on the humidity, heat, exhaustion, or too much exercise that day.

"I'm tired of you always blaming your falls on something. Stop it. You're getting worse. No more excuses."

The truth pierced my ego and really hurt this time. Especially hearing it from Andrea. I knew Andrea had always been my voice of truth. This time was different. This truth really hurt. This truth forced me to wake up from my living nightmare and question my hope and positive attitude. Lying on the floor, legs motionless, not in control and completely dependent on someone else forced me to question my new reality. Why me? This sucked with no visible improvement in my future. I tried every possible therapy but kept getting worse. She knew it and so did I. What now? I had to dig deeper and find my last remnant of hope.

How could we make life easier at home? We had to solve the shower issue. We also had to solve the problem of getting into and out of our house. When I walked with a cane, we installed decorative handrails so I had something to hold onto going up or down the steps. When I started bring my scooter into our house, I bought three ramps to negotiate the three sets of steps and threshold through our front door. The ramps worked great with the scooter since I drove the three wheeled machine in a relative straight line. However, one afternoon the skies filled with lightning, thunder and lots of rain. It poured. Jacob called me to pick him up from school. While I knew I would get wet, I turned too quickly on the final ramp and drove off the ramp's side lip. My scooter tipped over and my hands hit the driveway like shock absorbers before the fall. While I tried to figure out how to pick myself up, I became soaked from the downpour. My clothes felt very heavy. Thankfully a neighbor had seen it happen and helped me get back on the scooter. Unfortunately the rain shorted out the electrical system and forced me into my manual wheelchair. I cringed whenever I had to use the manual chair because it didn't fit through our doors and my lack of arm strength made it difficult to maneuver around the house. Once I took delivery of my electric wheelchair, I realized that the ramps were not wide enough to accommodate my erratic driving. I did not realize the joystick sensitivity could be reprogrammed to lessen the jerkiness of the forward motion. One day while leaving our house for Pilates class, my wheelchair fishtailed on my second ramp and I tipped over into our flowerbed with my three hundred eighty pound wheelchair on top of me. Two neighbors saw it happen and came to my rescue - again.

We had to solve these problems – and quickly. My paranoia over falling in and around our shower or driving off one of the ramps consumed my thoughts. Soon after we hired a contractor who specialized in accessible remodeling, we borrowed money from our variable life insurance policies to pay for this major expense. They reconfigured our master bathroom with a roll-in shower, widened three doorways, and added a door in our office connected to a platform lift into our garage. Most builders installed thirty-inch doors in new houses. While we had the foresight to build a house with a first floor master bedroom, we never anticipated my ability to walk would disappear. The doorways into our bedroom, bathroom and office caused me problems with my scooter and wheelchair. Many times I ran into these narrow doorjambs and sliced open my kneecaps. Thirty-six inch doors solved the problem in our office and master bedroom. We also installed a thirty-six inch pocket door in our master bathroom that created more room to enter and exit without any worry of running into the door in the middle of the night. The vertical platform lift provided me a safe solution to enter and exit our garage without exposure to inclement weather. Thankfully, we identified and solved another set of problems.

This latest problem solving episode felt like the story of my life. Unfortunately, my story proved to have mixed results. For someone who always wanted to be proactive and stay ahead of my disease progression, I found myself reacting to issues created from this ugly disease. The tension from this conflict increased with the passage of time. Periodically I've seen friends or former colleagues at sports events, concerts and restaurants. "David, it's great to see you. You look great!" After hearing their words, I often thought to myself, "What did they expect to see?" If someone called me on the telephone, they would never know I had MS. In-person visits allowed them the luxury of seeing my wheelchair and asking about my disability. Either way, they spoke to or saw the same person. My mind worked fine. My legs didn't.

Once again, I reflected back to my trip to Brazil. Am I glad I went? Did it help meeting John of God, the spiritual healer? What great questions. Did he cure me? No, absolutely not. In the Winter 2008 issue of Inform MS, an article written by Karen Wenzel piqued my interest. She wrote, "A cure is a treatment that removes all evidence of a disease or pathology. Healing, in contrast, is an internal process of reorganization that promotes a sense of being intact, undiminished and whole. Healing can take place on a physical, emotional or spiritual level. While there is not yet a cure for MS, there are multiple opportunities for healing."

Did John of God heal me? Absolutely. I believed he or one of the entities healed me on a spiritual level. My attitude had always been positive and very strong. When I returned from Brazil, I knew I would walk again. My conviction and purpose towards life improved beyond measure. I felt a new sense of being with a strong belief in myself. My ability to turn spiritual strength into demonstrated physical gains became my baseline for future personal growth.

Attitude and hope drove my personal inspiration. Everyone always told me they had never met someone with such a positive attitude. One evening after dinner, Jacob and I watched CSI on TV. During a commercial break, an advertisement ran about anti-depressants. "Dad, are you depressed? Do you take an anti-depressant?"

"Jacob, that's a very good question. If anyone should be depressed it should be me. I've read that not being able to sleep at night can be a symptom of depression. My body always feels tired but I can't sleep – even with sleeping pills. At night when it rains I can hear every rain drop. Life certainly dealt me a unique set of challenges. But I'm not depressed. I enjoy living life too much to be depressed. The only hint of depression in me comes while watching sad movies or TV episodes. Remember the year-end episode of Law and Order – Special Victims Unit? Elliot's wife was in labor on the way to the hospital in Olivia's car when a drunk driver slammed into them and trapped them in the car. The fire department used the jaws-of-life to cut them out. The tears poured from my eyes. In my opinion, I'm much more in touch with my emotions but not depressed. Going to Brazil helped me find my emotions and realize it's OK to let people see them. You, Sydney and Mom give me too much strength to be depressed. I look forward to every new day."

Several days later, Andrea and I sat at the breakfast table drinking our morning coffee. Andrea unexpectedly spoke while I turned the page of the Business Section. "I had a dream about you last night. We were on the beach holding hands while we walked. I asked you what happened to your wheelchair. You told me you left it behind us." Her words took me by surprise. Her dream confirmed my dreams. In all of my dreams, I never saw myself in a wheelchair. I knew I would walk again. Patti always told me you had to train your mind so your words became reality. Both of us seeing me walk confirmed I would walk again.

My purpose gained strength. I had new reasons to think positive thoughts. And then something totally unpredictable rocked my world. Jacob and I loaded into my van for his first soccer game of the season. He always helped me arrange my feet on the floor of the van once I transferred from my wheelchair. After placing my car into gear, something did not feel right in my left arm. I tried to turn the wheel when we circled around our cul-de-sac. Our neighbor worked in her front yard while I fumbled to slow the car to a stop with my hand controls. With all my strength, I pushed forward with my left hand on the hand controls to slow my van to a stop. While winded and out of breath, I acted as though I meant to stop. Luckily I stopped without running through their front yard. "Hi Donna. Thanks for helping with my transfer." Earlier in the week I almost fell to the floor while attempting to transfer from my wheelchair. I screamed for help. "Help. Help. Help. Can someone please help me?" With Donna running towards my van, our remodeling contractor came over and lifted me into the driver seat.

After pulling away from Donna's house, my left arm failed to push the hand control forward enough to slow the vehicle. While I tried to turn the car with my right hand, I ran over one of my neighbor's butterfly bushes in their front yard. My car proceeded to run through the large rocks that lined their next door neighbor's driveway. Somehow I managed to turn sharply and make the left turn from our cul-de-sac to the main road of our subdivision. Luckily there weren't any kids playing in the street because I popped the curb while yelling for Jacob to turn off the car. Big mistake. When he turned off the ignition, I lost power steering. I pushed on the hand controls really hard while attempting to slow down. We finally stopped by crashing into a flowerbed with a three-foot diameter rock wedged under my van. Somehow I missed the fire hydrant that sat inches from my right tire. After waiting two hours for a tow truck to pull us out, Donna's husband, Steve, drove my van back to our house. Luckily no one got hurt – no one except for my pride. I knew what had to happen. That day would be my last day driving a car. Unfortunately, my independence took a turn for the worse while my ego deflated.

During the two hours attempting to fall asleep that evening, I found myself visualizing the white marble staircase from my cellular cleaning. I walked down the stairs and once again saw the long narrow hallway at the bottom of the stairs. I walked through the darkened hall and turned to open the last door on the right. The room looked spotless like I left it three years ago. I walked into the room holding a can of royal blue paint in my right hand. The paintbrush rested on top of the can. I sat down in the far left corner of the room and started painting the floor. I kept scooting backward painting myself into the corner without any way out. Where do I go now?

Once again, I found myself reflecting on my life's journey since being diagnosed with MS ten years ago. The disease kept taking things away from me. I asked myself, "What do I really miss?" I missed taking long walks with Andrea, our hands interlocked. I missed walking. I missed yard work. I missed climbing the second floor steps to say goodnight to Sydney and Jacob. I missed camping and pleasure vacations. I missed going to friends houses for dinner without worrying how many steps they had in the front of their house. I missed playing beach volleyball. I missed using my education and training at work. I missed driving. I missed my independence. I missed sharing kid responsibilities with Andrea so she would not need to be in constant motion.

The more I thought of things I missed, the more the list grew. But I also felt thankful and blessed. I felt blessed with a loving wife and wonderful kids. I felt blessed to give back to others through mentoring and speaking on behalf of the National MS Society. I felt blessed that my hope and attitude gave me strength. I felt blessed that my family helped me live without any complaints. I felt blessed that I married an incredible woman. I felt blessed that I focused on what I could do and ignored those tasks I could no longer accomplish. Yes, life threw me a disproportionate share of challenges. Maybe these challenges were too many for most people to overcome. Not me. My hope and attitude helped me persevere because I knew in my heart that my health would improve.

The voice in the back of my head spoke loudly again. "Stop trying so hard. Give yourself a break and let go. You've been through enough. It's OK if you don't walk again. Why can't you accept things the way they are?" This voice sounded unfamiliar to me. Where did it come from? I cannot and will not listen to this voice. Not now, not ever.

My head shook violently from side to side. Those thoughts had to go away. I could not believe my mind even thought those thoughts. I would never give up. I knew I would walk again. My determination regained control after I saw my mom's face lying in her nursing home bed. She started speaking to me. This woman had created my stellar attitude and passion for life. This woman inspired me to fight back with hope. This woman had so much courage and smiled every day. This woman spoke the same words I heard from her so many times before: "D-a-v-i-d............ one day at a time!"

20

EPILOGUE

Stay positive. Remain hopeful. Keep trying. Never give up. These words define my personal mantra. While my thoughts and actions demonstrated my commitment to this mantra, many times my body had other plans. Sure I kept fighting. Sure I kept smiling with dreams of better days ahead. But anyone afflicted with this brutal disease will admit that unpredictable events force you to ask, "Here we go again, what's next?"

The month following my car debacle, my bladder revolted. Like every other morning, I raised the head of my bed using my adjustable bed's remote control. One leg at a time, I lifted and swung each of my legs onto the floor. Normally I grabbed the metal arm of my Superpole with my right hand, pushed off my bed with my left hand, stood up and ninety-degree pivoted into my wheelchair. This morning was different. After sitting on the edge of the bed, I had a tremendous urgency to urinate. Within seconds, my bladder uncontrollably drained onto our hardwood floor. Since Andrea was out-of-town, I had to ask Sydney to clean up the mess before she left for school. How embarrassing.

Three days later, my Urologist's Physician Assistant recommended I self-catheterize after urinating before bedtime. She concluded I wasn't completely emptying my bladder thus causing my bladder to be overfull when I woke-up in the morning. Her words made me cringe. The lack of dexterity in my hands, especially my left hand, meant Andrea had to perform the procedure every night. What a nightmare. This effort went above and beyond what any spouse should have to endure in the name of love. Andrea and I looked at each other before she said, "Show me what to do. If this can solve David's problem, I will do it."

All I could do was look down at the floor and shake my head. Andrea never ceased to amaze me. My life-long partner once again demonstrated her commitment to me without a second thought. She really was an angel.

Nine days later, my world imploded. Andrea left early in the morning as she always did on Wednesdays for her networking breakfast. After we kissed and wished each other to have a great day, I began my ritual of standing up and ninety-degree pivoting onto the bathroom toilet using PT bars to lift me up with my arm strength prior to transferring my weight to my legs. Normally I accomplished the transfer on the first attempt. This morning it took seven attempts. Winded and out of breath, something didn't feel right. I felt really weak; sweat poured from my forehead, and could not catch my breath. For four long hours I yelled for help but no one could hear me. My cell phone was unreachable in the pocket on the other side of my wheelchair. I couldn't lift my arms or move any part of my body. My yells for help got fainter as the paralysis increased. Please help me, anybody.

Finally, I heard the door open and shut in our laundry room. I yelled with my last ounce of strength, "Andrea, please help me. You need to call 911. I'm in big trouble."

She ran towards my voice. "Oh my God. What's wrong? Have you been sitting there the whole time I've been gone?"

Within five minutes, two paramedics and four firemen rushed into our house. First they asked me a bunch of medical history questions. Then they took my vital signs. My pulse was 133, temperature 103.5 and my blood pressure was extremely low. How could this happen to me? Why me again? Why am I paralyzed? Thank God Andrea came home when she did. My mind raced through feelings like scared, relieved, exhausted, confused and afraid to let go of life. All I could do was close my eyes and hope for a positive outcome.

It took four men to lift me onto their stretcher. Tears formed at the corners of my eyes. I couldn't lift or move my hands or toes and felt sorry for myself. Am I going to die? The paramedic in the ambulance kept asking me questions on the ride to the hospital. My answers came from someone else in my mind. I was so scared and thoughts of losing my family overwhelmed my words and me. Once we arrived at University Hospital's Emergency Room, a nurse parked me in their hallway. I pleaded for a room because I desperately needed to urinate after five long hours of bladder inactivity. After my nurse inserted a Foley catheter and started a broad-spectrum antibiotic through an IV tube in my arm, I had to wait for my blood test results. The ER nurse told me they planned to admit me into the hospital once they had an available room. My ER room had no windows, no TV, and no telephone.

After forty-four excruciating and boring hours, the admitting nurse found me a room. Thank God. I couldn't sleep all night because of a drug addict they brought to the ER at 1:00 AM. All night long this lady screamed, "Help me, somebody please help me." Her cries for help were really about her wanting drugs, any drugs. Finally morning arrived. Coincidentally, the same time a kitchen worker delivered my breakfast tray, eight energetic women walked into my room. Their supervisor explained they were nursing students working their clinical rotation in the ER. "What can they do to help you?"

"I can't move my arms. Can they help me eat?"

"Absolutely. How about a sponge bath? They can also change your sheets and gown. Is that OK with you? They need the practice."

For the first time in two days I smiled. Seven female nursing students could give me a sponge bath any day of the week!

Within an hour after transferring to my room on the Neurology Floor, another doctor walked in and introduced himself as the Team Leader of the Rehab Unit. We discussed my medical history and the events that led me to the hospital. "First, I wanted to let you know you have a urinary tract infection, also called a UTI. The reason I'm here is because we have a bed open on our floor. We are very selective about who we admit into this Unit because we want our patients motivated to get better. You know, someone who will work hard and fight through our "Boot Camp" that includes three hours per day of PT and OT with a positive attitude."

Is this guy for real? Am I worthy? "Doctor, you will never meet anyone with a stronger attitude who is more motivated than me. I know I am going to walk again. There is no doubt in my mind. When can I start?"

For the next nine days, I worked really hard trying to regain my strength back to my former baseline pre-hospitalization. Before boot camp, I had 50% functionality in my left arm and I could stand and pivot for transfers to and from my wheelchair. While I tried and fought to reach my former baseline, I had to swallow hard and accept my new reality. My baseline shifted lower because my body weakened from the infection. Now I needed to use a slide board instead of standing for transfers and only had 25% functionality in my left arm. My disease must be progressing. Why did God keep testing my resilience?

So be it – for now. After my discharge, the home care provider scheduled PT and OT visits 3-4 days per week. I worked really hard. Why did this sound so familiar? Day after day I fought to regain my strength. Two months later, I returned for an appointment with my Urologist. After several tests on my bladder, my doctor agreed to insert a supra–pubic catheter. The following week I returned to the hospital for this minor surgery. Finally, I solved another inconvenience. Now I could go anywhere I needed to go without worrying about how I would transfer to a toilet in someone's house or at a restaurant.

Thirty days after my surgery, my doctor asked me to return to the hospital so his staff could train Andrea to change my catheter. It was a very simple procedure. Two days later, I regretted this doctor appointment. It became very hard to breathe and my temperature increased to a worrisome level. I couldn't believe it, another trip to the hospital. Luckily, we had just finished dinner so we drove to a hospital closer to our house. After several blood tests, the emergency room doctors concluded I developed a urinary tract infection. I was so mad. The only way I could catch an infection was at the hospital when they changed my catheter. I thought hospitals were supposed to be sterile.

Infections and me didn't get along very well. Every time infectious bacteria entered my body, paralysis crippled me and I couldn't move. One mistake we made by choosing this hospital related to them not having a Rehabilitation Unit. After five long days in the hospital, they discharged me and once again recommended home care for physical and occupational therapy. Unbelievable. Same story different verse. The infection predictably weakened my entire body. My baseline shifted lower again, especially in my left arm. Now I only had 10% functionality. Keep fighting. Keep smiling. Don't give up. The voice in the back of my head screamed loudly again, "Remember, the alternative is unacceptable."

After two months religiously working hard 3 to 4 days a week with my therapists, they both suggested it was time to discharge me and begin outpatient therapy at the Colorado Neurological Institute. My PT's name was Dottie. Not only did she help me regain my strength, Dottie also probed for ways to make life easier for Andrea and me. "Do you have any other types of insurance like long-term care insurance?" I had never really thought about it. When I worked at Marsh, I enrolled in a long-term care program offered by MetLife. At the time, I viewed this insurance as nursing home coverage. After calling MetLife, they told me my policy covered homecare if I could not perform three out of six daily functions such as dressing, bathing, eating, toileting, transferring (getting in and out of a bed or chair), and walking.

Amazing. After several weeks of paperwork, MetLife approved me for daily visits by a Certified Nursing Assistant (CNA). What a relief. Now I didn't have to bother Andrea to help me take a shower, make my lunches, or take me to my numerous doctor appointments. Between driving to and from kid activities and working at our framing store, Andrea never had any free time. Now I could make life easier for her.

My CNA came five days a week and helped me exercise, stretch, and get out of bed on days when Andrea attended an exercise class at 5:30 AM on Tuesdays and Fridays. Life started feeling normal again. At least normal related to my world.

For the first time in many months, we decided to go out for breakfast on a Sunday morning. It felt good to do things as a family. We ate good food, laughed a lot, and told ourselves we needed to go back to this restaurant again. After we left, Andrea started my van and lowered my lift to the pavement. I backed onto the lift and asked Andrea to lift me up. When I reached the top, I didn't feel very comfortable the way I sat on my chair cushion. While leaning forward to push myself back on my seat, everything became dreamlike in slow motion. Because I leaned too far forward, my body weight flipped my chair and me off the lift three feet down onto the pavement. The next thing I knew, I crashed to the pavement with my body weight plus my chair - approximately 575 pounds. With all that weight, my left ear followed by my hands became the contact points. Another nightmare rocked my world in broad daylight.

Once Andrea realized what happened, she ran around the van and saw me lying on the ground with my wheelchair on top of me. The first thing she did was look into my ear to see if my brain was leaking cerebral fluid. "Andrea, did I crack my head open?" Tears flowed from my eyes. The pain overwhelmed me. Thankfully, Andrea did not see any brain fluids; only blood from the cuts in and on my ear. I cried out in pain when she cleaned the abrasions with gauze and alcohol. My left ear had already swelled to three times the size of my right ear. Two men quickly ran over and helped me sit up in my chair.

Every time I told this story, friends and neighbors looked totally shocked, especially when they looked at my ear. Everyone fired questions at me. "Did an ambulance come?" "How long were you in the emergency room?" People could not believe I didn't crack my head open or break my neck. Me too. Looking into their eyes, my response always took them aback. "We never went to the emergency room. I figuratively walked away with no major structural damage. Imagine that! God is not finished with me. He has more for me to accomplish." Then I smiled.

The following month, I surprised Andrea with a special 50th birthday present. She and her sister Laura traveled for ten days throughout Italy. They spent four days in Rome, three in Florence, and three days along the Amalfi Coast. It gave me so much pleasure to let her get away and travel abroad. Internally, sending Andrea away on a once in a lifetime dream trip without me tore me up. I should be on that trip with my best friend and soul mate. It just wasn't fair. I knew my body couldn't travel that far in a non-ADA compliant country, but I wanted to be the one sharing those memories with Andrea. This was just another example of MS taking something immeasurable away from me. Oh well, so be it. Both Andrea and her sister had an amazing time on their trip. That's what mattered most to me. Her pictures, endless smiles, and time away having fun dwarfed my sadness. In the name of love, seeing Andrea happy was all that mattered.

Two days after Andrea returned home, I called her at our frame store about an hour after finishing my lunch. "Hi there. I've got a question for you. Where are your kidneys located relative to your lungs?"

Andrea replied, "Your kidneys are below your lungs near your pelvis. Why do you ask? Is something wrong?"

"Well, I don't know. After lunch I started working on the computer and I noticed a sharp pain in my side near my right lung. Now I'm having problems breathing. What should I do?"

"It sounds like a pulmonary embolism, also known as a blood clot. I'm going to call Dr. Weller and schedule an appointment for you this afternoon. Count on me being home shortly."

An hour later, Andrea walked through our laundry room door to our garage. "Your appointment is set for 3:30 PM. "How do you feel?"

"I can't wait another ninety minutes. Please call them back and cancel. The pain in my side really hurts and I can't catch my breath. We need to go to the emergency room now. Dr. Weller would send me there anyway."

Ten minutes later, I laid on a hospital gurney in the ER closest to our house. It took four different nurses nine times to find a vein acceptable for an IV catheter. My patience started wearing very thin. Finally, one of the nurses connected me to their oxygen because I couldn't catch my breath. My pain kept increasing on my right side. "Andrea, what's wrong with me? I'm really afraid."

Unexpectedly, tears started pouring from my eyes. I was afraid, frustrated, feeling sorry for myself, and losing control. Frustration tears, that's what came out. Here I am, flat on my back in another hospital for the third time in ten months. I've done everything right through fighting back with exercising, making life safer and easier on Andrea, and keeping a positive attitude. The tears kept flowing. I had found the trough of sadness and desperation. Am I going to die?

My thoughts gave way to an unending barrage of tests. First, technicians performed a chest x-ray to check for pneumonia. Next, two individuals took me away for a CAT-scan of my mid-section to locate the blood clot. Finally, another group of technicians used sonogram equipment on my legs looking for additional blood clots before they could move to my lungs or heart.

Back in my room, the nurse disconnected my portable oxygen tank and reconnected me to the supply line in the room. An ER doctor walked into the room. "Doctor, please tell me what's going on in my body."

"Your chest x-ray shows you have pneumonia. The CAT scan located a blood clot in your lower right lobe of your lung. You are very lucky you came to us when you did. Had you waited much longer, the clot could have traveled through your heart and then your brain. Both of those scenarios lead to fatalities. You are very lucky to be alive. We're starting you on strong IV antibiotics and heparin to start thinning your blood. The nurses should move you soon to a room."

It took three days to stabilize me enough to transfer by ambulance to Swedish Medical Center's Rehab Unit. Excellent. Now I could focus on getting stronger as my body began to wake up. How strange. I actually looked forward to the three hours of intensive PT and OT every day. The therapists and nurses could not believe my attitude towards regaining my strength and feeling better. Nurses repeatedly came into my room to hear my story of always fighting back with a positive attitude. It perplexed me that most patients they provided care to did not respond like me with such conviction.

On my last night in the Unit, a nurse walked into my room and sat next to me. "David, you are amazing. After all you have endured, you continue to smile and work really hard to improve the quality of your life. So many people who transfer to our floor complain and give up on getting better. You are an inspiration to all of us."

We hugged as tears formed in the corners of our eyes. It felt so good to hear her words. I had to keep fighting. No doubt in my mind.

One month after returning home, Andrea and I took Jacob to his student-led parent teacher conference. I liked meeting Jacob and Sydney's teachers and hearing their progress in school. We walked into his English class and met his teacher, Ms. Wickstrom. Jacob found his folder of class work and showed us his writing assignments and told us why they were important. After finishing with another student and her parents, his teacher asked us if we wanted to see Jacob's latest assignment. Andrea and I both responded, "Of course we do."

"I provided the students with a prompt from "This I Believe," which is an NPR lesson, that invites writers from around the world to share their personal beliefs and philosophies about life. Go to the website, www.thisibelieve.org, and you can learn all about it. It has high school and middle school curriculum, too, but there are thousands of wonderful essays just like Jacob's. Here it is, I think you'll enjoy it."

This, I believe

If you've ever seen a movie or television show where there is a young kid, they're always playing catch with their dad outside. In a perfect world, every kid would get to share this quality time with his or her parent. Frankly, this isn't a perfect world. If it were, I would have memories of my dad and I playing catch or tag. But my dad has multiple sclerosis. MS is a disease that affects the brain and prevents the body from doing certain things. In my dad's case, he can't walk and doesn't have much function in his arms. He can't do some things other dads can do. It may be things like driving, making lunch or even getting dressed. It's not about the things he can't do; it's the things he can do. This, I believe: cherish the simple things in life.

I do have to help my dad with things like brushing his teeth and picking up things he has dropped. I don't look at it as if it was a bad thing but I see other qualities he has. For example, he is always there for my sister and me. He can still help us with our homework or give us advice about friendship. You have to see past his wheelchair and other equipment he uses throughout the day. My dad is still the same guy inside as every other adult male I know. He still has a sense of humor and still likes to watch football on the weekends. The good thing is that he's able to see past his handicap too. His hope is what gets him out of bed in the morning. The attitude he has rubs off onto everyone he knows, including me.

If you are always looking at the negatives in life and never the positives, there's no point. Life isn't enjoyable. My dad may be in a wheelchair, but he is the coolest guy I know. If you just see past the first glance judgment, you'll see it too. You can't take the simple things in life for granted because you'll never know if you might lose it, especially when you know someone who has lost something you have.

Oh my God. My eyes welled up with tears and had to read his essay again. Jacob made me feel so proud. He totally understood that a wheelchair or any disability does not define a person. My legs might not work – yet – but my mind stays sharp and positive. It doesn't matter that I typed the last 80 pages of this book with the pinkie finger of my right hand. I accept my condition but know everything will improve. My health will improve because I want it to improve. I will walk again because I want to walk again.

So here I am, loving life for all the right reasons. I am so happy I retired from the daily grind of working every day. My relationship with Sydney and Jacob is stronger than ever. Staying home every day affords me the luxury of being a part of their crazy teenage years. Andrea and I love each other on a much deeper level until death do us part. My disability checks from The Hartford and Social Security provide income stability to live our lives comfortably. I can honestly say I am fulfilling my roles as a parent, husband and provider.

With all that said, I am ready for more. I am ready to walk again, hold Andrea's hand on long walks, play beach volleyball, take vacations to exotic destinations, stand up and hug people with both arms, drive again, and help other people realize they can overcome adversity in any form thrown before them. Who knows, maybe I'll even go back to work again. My mom's voice enters my thoughts. "David, remember, one day at a time." We smile, hug, kiss each other on the cheek and walk away!